Contemporary Irish Writers

Conor McPherson
Imagining Mischief

Gerald C. Wood

The Liffey Press

Published by The Liffey Press
Ashbrook House, 10 Main Street,
Raheny, Dublin 5, Ireland.
www.theliffeypress.com

© 2003 Gerald C. Wood

A catalogue record of this book is
available from the British Library.

ISBN 1-904148-11-5

All rights reserved. No part of this publication may be
reproduced or transmitted in any form or by any means,
including photocopying and recording, without written
permission of the publisher. Such written permission must also
be obtained before any part of this publication is stored in a
retrieval system of any nature. Requests for permission should
be directed to: The Liffey Press, Ashbrook House,
10 Main Street, Raheny, Dublin 5, Ireland.

Printed in the Republic of Ireland by ColourBooks Ltd.

Contemporary Irish Writers and Filmmakers

General Series Editor:
Eugene O'Brien, Head of English Department,
Mary Immaculate College, University of Limerick.

Titles in the series:

Seamus Heaney: Creating Irelands of the Mind
by Eugene O'Brien (Mary Immaculate College, Limerick)

Brian Friel: Decoding the Language of the Tribe
by Tony Corbett

Jim Sheridan: Framing the Nation by Ruth Barton
(University College Dublin)

John Banville: Exploring Fictions by Derek Hand
(St. Patrick's College, Drumcondra, Dublin)

Neil Jordan: Exploring Boundaries by Emer Rockett and
Kevin Rockett (Trinity College Dublin)

Roddy Doyle: Raining on the Parade by Dermot McCarthy
(Huron University College, University of Western Ontario)

Conor McPherson: Imagining Mischief by Gerald Wood
(Carson-Newman College, Tennessee)

William Trevor: Re-imagining Ireland by Mary Fitzgerald-Hoyt
(Siena College, New York)

Forthcoming:

Jennifer Johnston by Shawn O'Hare
Brian Moore by Philip O'Neill
John McGahern by Eamonn Maher
Brendan Kennelly by John McDonagh

Contents

About the Author

Gerald C. Wood has written articles in the United States on various topics in literature and film, including Lord Byron and satire, the horror film, and movie versions of American history. The focus of his recent work has been Horton Foote, the playwright and filmmaker who won Academy Awards for *To Kill a Mockingbird* (1963) and *Tender Mercies* (1982) as well as the Pulitzer Prize for his play *The Young Man from Atlanta* (1995). Wood edited a collection of Foote's one-act plays for Southern Methodist University Press (1989) and *Horton Foote: A Casebook*, from Garland Press in 1998. His critical study *Horton Foote and the Theater of Intimacy*, published by Louisiana State University Press the following year, was nominated for both the George Jean Nathan and the C. Hugh Holman awards. The author is Professor and Chair of English at Carson-Newman College in Jefferson City, Tennessee, where he also serves as film editor of *Nua: Studies in Contemporary Irish Writing*.

Series Introduction

Given the amount of study that the topic of Irish writing, and increasingly Irish film, has generated, perhaps the first task of a series entitled *Contemporary Irish Writers and Filmmakers* is to justify its existence in a time of diminishing rainforests. As Declan Kiberd's *Irish Classics* has shown, Ireland has produced a great variety of writers who have influenced indigenous, and indeed, world culture, and there are innumerable books devoted to the study of the works of Yeats, Joyce and Beckett. These writers spoke out of a particular Irish culture, and also transcended that culture to speak to the Anglophone world, and beyond.

However, Ireland is now a very different place from that which figures in the works of Yeats, Joyce and Beckett, and it seems timely that the representations of this more secular, more European, and more cosmopolitan Ireland should be investigated and it is with this in mind that *Contemporary Irish Writers and Filmmakers* has been launched.

This series will examine the work of writers and filmmakers who have engaged with the contemporary cultural issues that are important in Ireland today. Irish literature and film has often been viewed as obsessed with the past, but contemporary writers and filmmakers seem to be involved in a process of negotiation between the Ireland of the past and the Ireland of the coming times. It is on this process of negotiation that much of our current imaginative literature and film is focused, and this series hopes to investigate this process through the chosen *auteurs*.

Indeed, it is a sign of the maturity of these *auteurs* that many of them base their narratives not only in the setting of this "new Ireland", but often beyond these shores. Writers and filmmakers such as Seamus Heaney, John Banville, William Trevor and Neil Jordan have the confidence to write and work as *artists* without the necessary addendum of the qualifying "Irish". Their concerns, themes and settings take them outside Ireland to a global stage. Yet, as this series attests, their "Irishness", however that is defined, remains intact and is often imprinted even in their most "international" works.

Politically and culturally, contemporary Ireland is in something of a values deficit as the previous hegemonic certainties of party political and religious allegiance have been lost in a plethora of scandals involving church and state. The role of art and culture in redefining the value-ethic for our culture has never been more important, and these studies will focus on the notions of Irishness and identity that prevail in the late twentieth and early twenty-first centuries.

The role of the aesthetic in the shaping of attitudes and opinions cannot be understated and these books will attempt to understand the transformative potential of the work of the artist in the context of the ongoing redefinition of society and culture. The current proliferation of writers and filmmakers of the highest quality can be taken as an index of the growing confidence of this society, and of the desire to enunciate that confidence. However, as Luke Gibbons has put it: "a people has not found its voice until it has expressed itself, not only in a body of creative works, but also in a body of critical works", and *Contemporary Irish Writers and Filmmakers* is part of such an attempt to find that voice.

Aimed at the student and general reader alike, it is hoped that the series will play its part in enabling our continuing participation in the great humanistic project of understanding ourselves and others.

Eugene O'Brien
Department of English
Mary Immaculate College
University of Limerick

Acknowledgements

When Geraldine Page received her only Academy Award, for her performance in *The Trip to Bountiful*, she said to the screenwriter Horton Foote, "It's all your fault, Horton." In the same spirit, I feel this book is the fault of Shawn O'Hare, who suggested to Eugene O'Brien that I be considered for this pleasant task. Although Shawn should not be held accountable for any eejitries which have crept into the following pages, I want to thank him for his confidence and initiative. In the same breath, I want to thank two other colleagues at Carson-Newman College, Andy Hazucha and John Wells, for their encouragement and understanding on our recent trips to Ireland. During my physical and emotional absences in pursuit of this project, they handled many student crises that should have been my responsibility. Worse yet, I didn't always pay for my share of the rounds while I was researching and writing this book. Thanks, my friends.

I want to thank Eugene O'Brien for accepting an out-of-the-blue e-mail. His enthusiasm for Conor McPherson's work was inspirational. At The Liffey Press, of course, I appreciate David Givens and Brian Langan for their many kindnesses, not the least of which was their willingness to support a Yank's interest in so controversial a young playwright.

In the States, I want to thank Nancy Friedland of Columbia University for sharing her knowledge of theatre and expert abilities as a researcher. As this work developed, she offered many useful questions and insights, as well as her growing appreciation for McPherson's work. At Carson-Newman College, I am indebted, as always, to Don Olive, Dean of Humanities, whose encouragement is felt in everything I do in the English Department. Bruce Kocour and Sheila Gaines helped with many thorny research issues; skilled librarians, they retrieved materials in ways still mysterious to me. My student assistant, Emily Hester, did A+ work in all tasks required by this project: research, abstracting, typing and proofing. You were brilliant, Emily. Thanks, too, to Nichole Stewart and Edra Garrett for many editorial tasks and thoughtful suggestions, and Chris Rhodes and Becky Boatwright for handling the many financial details of such a project. I appreciate every member of the English Department for tolerating and understanding my absences, both physically and emotionally, while I obsessed over this book. Mark Seagroves, Anjanette Large and Nathan Miles gave needed technical support, and the administration of the College, led by Presidents Cordell Maddox and James Netherton, Provosts Mark Heinrich and Mike Arrington, and Associate Provost Don Good, was supportive in many ways.

Back in Dublin I want to thank Sunniva O'Flynn of the Irish Film Archives for making many movies available to me, both in Ireland and the United States. And Mary Sherlock for her many kind words and help with purchases on both sides of the Atlantic. At the UCD library, Debra McCann and others helped me examine McPherson's master's thesis.

Of course, most of all, I appreciate Conor McPherson for granting the interviews, entertaining some naïve questions, and generously sharing feelings and unpublished manuscripts. Thanks, Conor, for being good to me . . . and for buying the coffee.

For Horton Foote

Chronology

1971	On 6 August, Conor McPherson born in Dublin, Ireland, to Michael and Clare McPherson. He is the middle child of three, with sisters Karen (older) and Margaret (younger). Spends childhood years in Coolock.
1988	Enrols at University College Dublin (UCD), eventually reading in philosophy and literature. Also briefly studied psychology, graduating in 1991, when he begins postgraduate work in philosophy. As member of dramsoc at UCD writes first plays: *Taking Stock* (1989), *Michelle Pfeiffer* (1990), *Scenes Federal* (1991), *Inventing Fortune's Wheel* (1991).
1992	Forms Fly By Night Theatre Company with Peter MacDonald, Jason Byrne, Valerie Spelman, Kevin Hely and others. The group stages new plays at International Bar, Dublin, including McPherson's *Radio Play*. *Rum and Vodka* premiered at UCD in November.
1993	McPherson earns MA in Philosophy (Ethics) at UCD. Thesis titled "Logical Constraint and Practical Reasoning: On Attempted Refutations of Utilitarianism". *A Light in the Window of Industry* staged at International Bar by Fly By Night.

1994	Fly By Night presents *The Stars Lose Their Glory* at the International Bar and *The Good Thief* at City Arts Centre, Dublin, as *The Light of Jesus*, in April. In October, renamed *The Good Thief* when presented at Dublin Theatre Festival. Play receives the Stewart Parker Award.
1995	Begins writing *I Went Down* for Treasure Films. *This Lime Tree Bower* opens in September at Crypt Arts Centre, Dublin. Receives Meyer-Whitworth Award for Best New Play and George Devine Award for Best New Play in same year. Completes draft of *I Went Down* by December.
1996	In spring, completes revisions of *I Went Down. Lime Tree* moves to Bush Theatre, London, in July, giving play and author wider audience. Play eventually wins Thames TV Award and Guinness/National Theatre Ingenuity Award. McPherson also becomes Writer-in-Residence at the Bush Theatre, where he drafts *St. Nicholas*.
1997	*St Nicholas* premieres at Bush Theatre in February, directed by McPherson and starring Brian Cox. *The Weir* opens at Royal Court Theatre Upstairs in July. McPherson receives the *Evening Standard* Award for Outstanding New Playwright and London Critics' Circle Most Promising Playwright Award. *I Went Down* released as feature film, becomes most successful Irish independent film to date. Film wins award for Best New Screenplay at the San Sebastian Film Festival. Also CEC Award for Best Screenplay.
1998	In February, *The Weir* moves to Royal Court Theatre Downstairs and is staged at the Gate Theatre, Dublin, in July. In March, *St Nicholas* opens in United States at Primary Stages, New York City. *I Went Down* is shown at the Sundance Film Festival in January and premiered in NYC in June.

1999	*The Weir* premieres in the US at Walter Kerr Theatre, New York. Wins Laurence Olivier BBC Award for Best New Play in London. Nominated for Outer Critics' Circle Award for Best Play in New York.
2000	*Dublin Carol* is premiered at Royal Court Theatre, London, in February. Play moves to Gate Theatre, Dublin, in October. It is nominated for both Best Production at the Dublin Theatre Festival and Best Play, Irish Times/ESB Award. Stages Cóilín O'Connor's *The Last Days of God* with Fly By Night. Also directs reading of Joe Penhall's *Blue/Orange* for Rough Magic Theatre Company, Dublin.
2001	*Port Authority* opens at New Ambassadors Theatre, London, in February. Moves to Gate Theatre, Dublin, in April. Both productions were directed by McPherson. *Saltwater* released. Receives CICAE Award for Best Film, Berlin Film Festival. McPherson's film of Samuel Beckett's *Endgame* included in Channel Four series *Beckett on Film*. *Come On Over* premieres in October at the Gate Theatre, Dublin, in evening of one-act plays with Brian Friel's *The Yalta Game* and Neil Jordan's *White Horses*. In December, directs Eugene O'Brien's *Eden* at Abbey Theatre, Dublin.
2002	Directs film *The Actors*, from own screenplay based on Neil Jordan story. Produced by Jordan.
2003	*Dublin Carol*, directed by McPherson, opens in February at Atlantic Theater Company, New York. In May, *The Actors* released in Ireland.

Abbreviations

A:	*The Actors*
COO:	*Come On Over*
DC:	*Dublin Carol*
GT:	*The Good Thief*
IWD:	*I Went Down* (published shooting script and commentary)
LCAPR:	"Logical Constraint and Practical Reasoning: On Attempted Refutations of Utilitarianism" (McPherson's UCD Thesis)
PA:	*Port Authority*
RAV:	*Rum and Vodka*
S:	*Saltwater* (published shooting script and commentary)
SN:	*St Nicholas*
TLTB:	*This Lime Tree Bower*
TWAOP:	*The Weir and Other Plays* (book published by Theater Communications Group, which includes, in addition to *The Weir, Rum and Vodka, The Good Thief, This Lime Tree Bower*, and *St Nicholas*)
W:	*The Weir*

Chapter One

Introduction: Monologues, Ensembles and Movies

Conor McPherson is the most successful of a new generation of Irish playwrights, which includes, among others, Martin McDonagh, Sebastian Barry, Marina Carr, and Billy Roche. Of this group, McPherson is noted as possessing an "amazing gift for storytelling" (Gamerman, 1999a: A20), often expressed in the monologue form. His most famous play, *The Weir*, studies the effect of ghost stories on a group of four men and a woman in a rural Irish pub. Whether monologue or ensemble, his writing uses "understatement, indirection and contained tenseness" to serve his "uncanny gift for getting inside the minds of the characters he creates" (Brantley, 2001: B5; Gamerman, 2001: A20). In the process he also challenges traditional definitions of theatrical experience. Repeatedly the characters attend to the audience, by acknowledging their presence, casting subtle glances, or even addressing them directly.

While some critics feel his monologues lack essential theatricality, McPherson believes he is exploring the playfulness of all theatre:

> I love the intimacy of somebody just confiding directly
> with you and the game that's being played in doing so.
> You know that it's just an actor but at the same time
> you want to believe what you're being told. You want
> it to be real. [. . .] What you establish is a sense of
> community between the audience, the actor and the
> writer whereby [. . .] everybody has imagined it and
> used pieces of their own life to make bits of the story
> work for themselves (Carty, 2000a: 2).

This reliance on a shared sense of narrative is the signature of
McPherson's drama:

> There is no theatrical fiction, no pretence that the
> stage represents an imaginary elsewhere. The time is
> now and the place is right here — in the theatre. The
> only character is the narrator — or narrators in the
> case of *This Lime Tree Bower* — and all he does is tell
> his story, without impersonating other characters or
> engaging in other physical histrionics. (Cummings,
> 2000: 304)

Such dedramatisation in favour of the story itself is the basis
of McPherson's achievement to date, even as he has moved
into writing and directing for film.

Conor McPherson began writing plays while an undergraduate student of English and philosophy at University College Dublin. His first work, still unpublished, imitated the
satiric style of American playwrights like Arthur Miller and
David Mamet. As McPherson has said, when he saw Mamet's
Sexual Perversity in Chicago as a first-year student at UCD,

> It was a massive eye-opener. Just to see all that
> swearing and to realise that it's legitimate. It made me
> think differently about writing and what people
> thought was acceptable. I became very interested in
> the way people speak and in how to replicate that. It

became my first impetus to try to write for the stage.
(Carty, 2000a: 2)

While McPherson's initial work received some good reviews
in Dublin, the writer was not satisfied with the "very fast dialogue about businessmen in shirt-sleeves" of early work like
Taking Stock (Gussow, 1999: B3).

He realised his distinctive voice and style when he started
experimenting with the monologue, the subject of Chapter
Two of this book. With the production of *Rum and Vodka*,
McPherson felt liberated by "the simplicity of it and the images
that people are creating themselves. In three sentences you
can convey a whole day." He had discovered, he felt, "a cinematic way of thinking" in which the speaker "can take an audience anywhere and describe anything. [. . .] You can jump
from someone's inner feeling to the actuality of the outer description of their circumstances" (Gussow, 1999: B3; Carty,
2000a: 2). Such freedom eventually inspired the playwright to
partially deconstruct the theatre by reminding the audience of
an obvious truth. "Why mess about?" he says. "The character
is *on stage*, perfectly aware that he is talking to a group of
people" (McPherson, 1996, "Author's Note" to *TLTB*, 5).

Such plays, according to McPherson, "work best when
kept conversational, understated. That's what makes them
believable. The temptation may be to launch into a one man
'performance', to 'act things out'. But such a performance will
never be as interesting as one where the actor trusts the
story to do the work" (McPherson, 1996, "Author's Note" to
TLTB, 5). Utilising such trust, an actor alone on the stage can
become the agent of what the playwright names dramatic
"mischief". In *St Nicholas*, as McPherson explains:

> with one actor talking only to the audience, what we
> have in front of us is a guide. He's telling us about
> somewhere outside the theatre, not trying to recre-
> ate it indoors. The theatre is simply where we meet

him. And if it's good we're reminded that we are in the theatre and we like being there.

And that's full of mischief because we collude with the actor in a very direct way. Especially when we have a well-known actor in front of us pretending to be someone else in a small theatre. It's a case of "Who's fooling who here?" And that can be a very rich and liberating experience. Because we've all started playing. (McPherson, 1999e, "Author's Note" to *SN*, 75–76)

However, as the playwright is quick to clarify, his mischievous theatre is not anarchic; it does not subscribe to, for example, the dehumanisation of art. Its goal is reflection inspired by reason:

Just as children's playing is often a rehearsal for adult life and dealings, so our theatrical grown-up playing has its serious intents. Because we are reflective beings and we like neatness. We want to know what everything *means*.

"What the hell am I supposed *to make* of this?" — that's us. That's what makes us responsible. And I think that's what *St Nicholas* might be about. The responsibility reason gives us. (McPherson, 1999e, "Author's Note" to *SN*, 76)

While liberated from theatrical conventions, the actors and audiences are not freed from either reason or responsibility. Despite his radical emphasis on the story, McPherson asks his players to reflect on life inside and outside the playhouse.

Such reflection is necessary in McPherson's most celebrated work, *The Weir*, which is discussed in Chapter Three. It is an "ensemble" play, as the author names it, dramatising the seductive nature of stories told by men in a lonely rural Irish pub. As they compete for the attention of Valerie, each in his own way hopes to have her to himself. But by the end of the play, such sharing of their stories has the opposite effect. They no longer see her simply as the object of their fantasies and desires. Once she tells of losing her daughter, Niamh, they begin to respond empathetically to her. As Jack says:

> Ah. Girl like you. Hiding yourself away. Listening to old headers like us talking about the fairies. Having all your worst fears confirmed for you. Tuh. Ghosts and angels and all this? Fuck them. I won't have it. Because I won't see someone like you being upset by it. You've enough to . . . deal with for fuck's sake. I am very, sorry, love, about what happened. (*TWAOP*, 68)

McPherson's film career had actually begun three years before *The Weir* was produced, though the writer wasn't aware of it at the time. In October of 1994, the Irish producer Robert Walpole and director Paddy Breathnach saw and were impressed by McPherson's second monologue, *The Good Thief*, which was playing in Dublin at the Theatre Festival. Within a year the filmmakers contacted the playwright about writing the original screenplay for *I Went Down*, which became the most successful independent Irish film to date (Power, 1999: 75; Kilroy, 2000: 5). Its story is described in the first section of Chapter Four. The second section of that chapter is devoted to McPherson's debut as a director with *Saltwater*, an adaptation of *This Lime Tree Bower*, the third of the monologues. Although not as commercially successful as *I Went Down*, *Saltwater* is a more personal study of the necessity of limiting mischief in order to achieve a balanced and responsible life, the quintessential McPherson subject. The fourth chapter also includes a brief description of the writer's adaptation of Samuel Beckett's *Endgame* and a preview of *The Actors*, which he directed for Neil Jordan in 2002, and *MacIntyre*, another project with Paddy Breathnach.

Because of the visual nature of his writing, film comes more easily to McPherson than many first-time filmmakers.

But he feels more comfortable in theatre, where the compromises are less substantial and the creator can keep more artistic control if he asserts himself (McKenzie, 2001a: par. 27). So, by the beginning of the new millennium, Conor McPherson returned to theatre with three new projects, which are discussed in Chapter Five. In *Dublin Carol*, he again used the ensemble. It is set in a real place, one outside the theatre — north Dublin — and follows traditional patterns of dramatic construction. But it also explores psychological issues and uses religious images unknown in previous McPherson plays. Such experimentation continued a year later when he allowed the multiple-monologue format to free itself of a central narrative. The result is his most poetic and religious theatre, *Port Authority*, a play resonant with unresolved feelings of loneliness. The fifth chapter concludes with McPherson's recent one-act play, *Come On Over*, his most abstract work.

While summarising the style and themes of McPherson's plays, Chapter Six also considers the degree to which he can be called a traditional Irish writer. Since Irishness is often misinterpreted, especially by critics with little knowledge of the increasing diversity of Irish culture and writing, McPherson's plays are often reduced to stereotypes. While his study of the "inner life" of his characters is, he believes, Irish, the writer feels free to explore more personally compelling topics. As Chapter Six explains, one such issue is the tension between the "laddish" characters and the writer's own preoccupation with ethical dilemmas. For Conor McPherson, even the least thoughtful or most confused of his characters eventually make defining choices. They become what they do. Whether in theatre or film, the writer asks his audiences to study the morality behind the obvious mischief. While McPherson has no agenda himself, and thus does not write with a moralistic imagination, his theatre turns on the dramatic moment when lives become a matter of morality.

Since Conor McPherson's plays are rarely staged outside Dublin, London and New York, many of his plays are unfamiliar to even the most avid theatregoers. The same is true of his films. As this book goes to print, his most personal film, *Saltwater*, has not been distributed to theatres or released on videotape in the US. In order to redress this problem, I have described the general style and plot of the plays and films. That was a difficult task because these works are often detailed, busy and outrageous; they have what Vincent Canby describes as "almost novelistic dimensions" (quoted in Renner, 1998: 21). In the case of the films, I have compared the published screenplays with the edited films, noting important variations appearing in the released movies. These summaries are followed by focused interpretations which place the individual works in the context of the McPherson canon. Following the discussions of individual works is an interview with McPherson, conducted in June and November of 2001. The book concludes with a bibliography of published works by the writer — essays, plays and films — and critical writing about his life and career. Even the concluding sections are driven by the desire to document the achievement of McPherson's complex art. Whether monologue, ensemble, or movie, his dramas are written at the intersection of Ireland's new economic and emotional freedoms and its ancient moral imperatives, both inside and outside the theatre.

Chapter Two

The Early Plays:
Rum and Vodka to *St Nicholas*

While he studied English and philosophy as an undergraduate at University College Dublin, Conor McPherson joined dramsoc, the student drama society. That very active group was responsible for producing his first four plays between 1988 and 1992: *Taking Stock* (1989), *Michelle Pfeiffer* (1990), *Scenes Federal (*1991), and *Inventing Fortune's Wheel* (1991). After his undergraduate degree in 1991, he continued with dramsoc while pursuing postgraduate work in philosophy, with emphasis on ethics. In 1992, he was one of the founding members of Fly By Night Theatre Company, which staged McPherson plays off the UCD campus, at Dublin venues like the International Bar. That is where *Radio Play, The Stars Lose Their Glory*, and A *Light in the Window of Industry* were first produced. Though these plays received some good reviews, the playwright considers them apprentice work and has no plans to restage or publish them.

According to McPherson, his artistry changed when he discovered the mischief in the monologue. As an English literature undergraduate at UCD, he would have read the dramatic monologue in poetry, especially as perfected by Robert

Browning. And he was probably familiar with the use of monologues as exercises in drama classes. A student of contemporary Irish theatre, he was about to observe Brian Friel returning in *Molly Sweeney* to the form which had inspired the seminal *Faith Healer* about fifteen years earlier. But the young Conor McPherson did not feel the burdens of any of this history — Irish or otherwise. For him, the monologue was personal and primitive. It freed him to explore his "quintessential" theme of loneliness and the essentials in drama — its "very roots", where it begins and ends — without regard for the conventions of theatrical construction (Cox, 1999: par. 19, 25). For the first time he could travel as freely as a novelist or filmmaker while indulging his narrators in wild flights to the boundaries of human civility and morality. After more than a half dozen tries, he was writing works he would claim as his own

Rum and Vodka

As Conor McPherson explains in his afterword to this play, published in *The Weir and Other Plays*, before he wrote *Rum and Vodka* he had written "normal ensemble plays with lots of characters talking to each other endlessly", plays clearly influenced by the work of David Mamet. These earliest works were, he confesses, "written with perhaps a sense of wanting to be a playwright rather than wanting to be a good writer". The writing of this play rescued him from such traditions and pretensions. While he retained the excesses of language and emotion inspired by Mamet's work, the monologue freed him from the seemingly endless, often pointless talk of the dialogue play. In *Rum and Vodka*, he believes, he "found [his] voice" (289).

McPherson wrote the play while completing his MA in philosophy at University College Dublin. He was twenty years old. It premiered at UCD on 27 November 1992, starring

Stephen Walshe and directed by the writer. *Rum and Vodka* was also performed at Trinity College and local Dublin venues before being staged at The City Arts Centre, Dublin, 30 August 1994, where it was directed by Cóilín O'Connor and performed by Jason Byrne. That production was under the auspices of the Fly By Night Theatre Company, co-founded by McPherson and some of his friends, including O'Connor, Byrne, Peter MacDonald, Valerie Spelman, and Kevin Hely (McPherson, 2000a: 12).

Rum and Vodka is in two "parts", implying that there is no acting in the traditional sense and thus no "acts". In the first, the narrator introduces himself as an impatient person whose irritability, lack of social graces, and pessimism stem from his inability to get answers to his questions. He says he and the rest of humanity are engaged in mutual hatred. But then, as he starts to analyse himself, he judges his explanations "a load of shit" and jumps into telling what's "happened to me over the last three days" (*TWAOP*, 244). He is twenty-four, married, and living in Raheny with his wife and two young daughters. He was married at twenty, he says, to a girl whom he got pregnant after a party. He then took a job "for the voting registration department of the Corporation on Wellington Quay", where his colleagues, Phil Comesky and Declan Short, seduced him into drinking excessively (244, 249). He believes Phil is unstable, evidenced by the story that Comesky once robbed the grave of a schoolboy for a buried love letter. Then, at three in the morning, he broke into the house of the girl who wrote it, wanting to read it to her.

Eventually, the unnamed narrator gets to the story he wants to tell. One Friday he is fired for drinking on the job and throws his computer terminal into the windscreen of his boss' car. He spends the rest of the night drinking with Phil, Declan, and their girlfriends. When he returns to his house, he has sex with Maria, his wife, while she is barely conscious. The next day, when they take the children, Carol and Niamh, to the shops, he anticipates a crisis when he can't pay the bill and so confesses that he has lost his job to his wife as they are driving the trolley through the aisles. Maria attacks him, the children cry, and he falls, toppling over another trolley, sending someone else's child skidding across the floor, banging its head on a shelf.

He flees the store and resumes his bar-hopping in Temple Bar, where he finds Phil and Declan at The Norseman pub. By ten o'clock, they continue at The Stag's Head, where they meet the girlfriends of Phil and Declan and the narrator spies a beautiful young woman with a trendy guy discussing his political play. Eventually the revellers are thrown out of the bar and continue on to the midnight show of Björn Again (an Abba tribute band) at the Olympia; after a half hour of the show, the narrator becomes bored and escapes to a bar, where he spots the girl from The Stag's Head and pleads with her to "Cure [his] life" (*TWAOP*, 268). After she helps him gain his composure in the ladies' toilet, they leave for her parents' house in Clontarf, where after another rum and vodka, he showers and they make love. She says her name is Myfanwy, a Welsh name.

Part two begins with another hangover. It is a quarter to ten, and he has regrets and is disgusted with the girl for being with a married man. He washes his clothes, takes paracetamol and a beer, and leaves the house for a pint and a short one. When he returns to Myfanwy's, he says his name is Michael, a lie, and she describes herself as a student at Trinity, reading business and Italian. He has sex with her not out of affection but to be able to keep drinking her alcohol. After she irons his clothes, they leave in her car for another pub, Davy Byrne's, where they have more drinks. She pays. He is now thinking of how long it will be until he needs more drink. They walk around Merrion Square and St Stephen's Green and finally eat on South Anne Street, at which point he begins speaking truthfully about his marriage and intentions. She is very accepting and willing to keep paying and seeing him.

At The International Bar, he calls one of her arty friends, Rupert, "a prick" (*TWAOP*, 282), but everyone thinks it is a joke. Myfanwy and the narrator walk the streets and then drive to her brother's house in Ranelagh, where she dresses him in her brother's expensive clothes and they have sex once again. They set out for a party at Rupert's, where there is a lot of drinking and smoking. After the narrator gets into a fight over a bottle of vodka, he discovers Myfanwy in a bedroom with Rupert, her shirt open while he performs oral sex on her as he masturbates. After taking £20 from Myfanwy's wallet, the speaker returns to his house, where he enters the quiet and is left sitting on the floor of his daughters' room listening to their breathing. *Rum and Vodka* ends with his confession: "I couldn't bear it" (288).

Rum and Vodka is a celebration of the monologue. In this first attempt at tackling that form, Conor McPherson revels in the details and the pace of the story being told. When the speaker and his wife fight in the grocery store, the specifics carry the action: "She hit me across the eye with a can of tuna. I think I blacked out. I tumbled backward into a freezer with Bird's Eye fishfingers and pizza and shit" (*TWAOP*, 259). These are the words and images of the sometimes evasive, sometimes inarticulate, sometimes cruel, sometimes charming McPherson monologist. He seems honest when he describes himself as a "pessimist" who lives without "answers", giving rise to his "lack of social graces" and paranoid feelings of disconnection and impotence:

> I think I hate the human race. And I think they know it. I often think the world gets together behind my back while I'm on the jacks or in bed and makes hasty decisions about new ways to get me to leave the planet. (243)

But he immediately neutralises the audience's judgement by calling his own words "the king of conspiracy theories" and "not true" (243). He freely admits to not liking himself, hating to look "back at things I've done", and "always doing something new", which creates "memories . . . like being different people". While not exactly a "load of shit", as he calls it, his self-explanation is forced, vague, and fascinating in its complexity (244). This is theatre, not the analytic couch.

The issue in this first play, like that in all of McPherson's early work, is the writer's attitude toward his narrator, the tone of the piece, and what effect this bizarre story has on the audience. A few reviewers, like Gerry McCarthy, believe McPherson demonstrates in *Rum and Vodka* his fascination with "the drink-driven excesses of lad culture" and "the booze-and-bird lifestyle, which is routinely contrasted with anything pretentious or middle-class" (2000a: 9). On the other hand, McPherson says he does not applaud his people; he writes "characters who a lot of the time either are so convinced of themselves that their arrogance is entertaining or [. . .] are sort of at a loss and really don't know what they're doing, so they just sort of strike out in a certain direction that ends up being disastrous" (Carty, 2000a: 2). This specific narrator, the writer reveals, is facing "the complete embarrassment of finding yourself in a position not of your own making. And it's your whole life" (White, 1994: 14, quoted in Cummings, 2000: 304). He feels like a victim, and McPherson asks the audience to decide if that is so.

The evidence supports McPherson's contention that he is not celebrating the life of his character. *Rum and Vodka*, despite the noise and protestations of its teller, is about the denial of responsibility for one's own life. At the Olympia, the narrator feels the impulse to "go down on the stage, grab a microphone and scream at everyone that none of what was happening to me was my fault" (*TWAOP*, 266). After spending the night with Myfanwy, he says she should have been less sluttish and more thoughtful of his wife, leaving himself guilt-less and free. As if to make the norms in the play explicit, when Myfanwy asks if he is still attracted to her, our speaker confesses, "she might as well have been talking about the Boer War as far as I held myself responsible" (277). He is fuelled by profound irresponsibility.

Even his most romantic impulses are tinged with this need to deny rather than engage his freedom and choices. Though driven by his need for alcohol, his obsession with the girl in the bar is initially an infantile desire to fuse with another person rather than control himself. First, he fantasises that when he would be with her he would have no worries; then, when he meets her, he pleads with her to "Cure my life. I want you to cure my life" (*TWAOP*, 263, 268). The real love of his life is drink. And it, like his erotic impulses, gives him a false self, one which denies the reality of his predicament: "I was glad of a drink. It took the edge off my worries. Brought out my self-reliance. If things are going well it helps you congratulate yourself. If you're in the shitter it gives you all the righteous indignation of an innocent victim" (253). Innocent victims don't need reason or self-control.

Like McPherson's most interesting characters, this narrator is at his best when he suggests emotions and conflicts that he does not understand, or at least will not betray, even when held captive by his audience. For example, his flight and alcoholic stupors camouflage the guilt and loss he feels toward his family. Before he arrives at The Stag's Head, he confesses: "As we left The Norseman I had a terrible feeling which I can only describe as homesickness. I suddenly wanted to play with the kids or have a bath with Maria sitting on the toilet talking to me" (*TWAOP*, 262). Less obviously, he projects the difficulties in his marriage onto the unhappy couple he meets at Rupert's party. Despite his inebriation, he tries to bring peace among them: "I wanted to know what was wrong with them. I wanted them to relax and cheer up. It sort of became important to me. They kept saying they were alright but I knew they were fucked. What was it about them? I don't know" (285). Not able to care for himself, he is anxious to become a caretaker of others.

Such "poetry of inarticulacy", as McPherson called it in an interview, is the most subtle comment the young playwright is making about his use of the monologue form in *Rum and Vodka* (Kilroy, 2000: 5). In most traditional plays, the performer articulates more clearly and decisively than people do in real life. But not so in his plays:

> What I really look for as a writer is to try and weave a sense of inarticulacy into my characters, because I think, in reality, people are sometimes not as articulate as a performer in a play. [. . .] What I try to do as a writer, I suppose, is try and evoke how difficult it is to communicate, and that is what I see as important to address (McKenzie, 2001a: par. 3).

The same observation is made by the narrator. When Rupert is droning on about acting school and Greek plays, the speaker interrupts him with a simple question: "I asked him what the theatre had to do with real life." Rupert's response is as unimpressive to the narrator as that made by practitioners of well-made drama would be to Conor McPherson: "I thought he'd have an answer seeing as he was at a school and everything. But he went on for about ten minutes and it was very boring. I can't remember what he said" (*TWAOP*, 280).

Rum and Vodka has the most literal title of McPherson's plays, whether they are monologues or ensembles. It is about alcohol and alcoholism. Typical of a McPherson play, it places the monologist in front of an audience who hears his ejaculations, confessions, evasions, failed attempts at communication, anxieties, hopes and fears. But he also says more than he knows or wills, freeing the audience to make their own judgements, none of which will be exactly the same. Some will find the obscenity funny; others will be put off. Some will pity him; others will lust for more vicarious thrills. But in this first monologue, McPherson has already established the dialectic. *Rum and Vodka*, like every play to follow, explores the dramatic territory between mischief and responsibility, both in the real world and through the illusions of the theatre, and asks the audience to make their own various and reasonable responses.

The Good Thief

McPherson's second monologue has a more suggestive, resonant title than *Rum and Vodka*. How it got that title, when the original one was *The Light of Jesus*, is both humorous and instructive:

> One day, walking down to the theatre, Garrett [Keogh, the actor, who is also McPherson's cousin] said, "You know no one is going to come and see a play called *The Light of Jesus*, don't you?" "Fuck them," I replied, all flushed and idealistic. All theatrical. We walked a little further in silence, down past Bewley's on Westmoreland Street. Then Garrett turned to me with a strange mixture of concern and amusement, "Do you know you're on ten per cent of the box office takings?" I had a little think, which led to a little mumble, "Well . . . I . . . had thought before about calling it . . . The . . . Good Thief." "Perfect," said Garrett. (*TWAOP*, 293)

According to the author, the political and financial realities mitigated his tendencies toward inflexible high-mindedness. Blood and friendship saved him from himself.

The play was first performed — as *The Light of Jesus* — at the City Arts Centre in Dublin, on 18 April 1994. Like the later performances of *Rum and Vodka*, the second monologue was produced by the Fly By Night Theatre Company. It was directed by the playwright and starred Kevin Hely, with slide photography by Paul Kinsella. On 4 October of that year, the play opened in the Dublin Theatre Festival as *The Good Thief*. The performance was produced by Loopline and designed by Anne Layde. While again directed by McPherson, it was acted by Garrett Keogh, with slide photography by Robbie Ryan. Later, the play also toured Ireland under the auspices of The Arts Council, without accompanying slides. Its American premiere was at the José Quintero Theatre in New York's East Village on 4 April 2001. That performance was directed by Carl Forsman and starred Brian d'Arcy James. It was produced by the Keen Company, with lighting by Josh Bradford and sound by Stefan Jacobs. The set was designed by Nathan Heverin, costumed by Theresa Squire and stage managed by Kara Bain.

The Good Thief is a single reading, with no intermission. Its once-again unnamed narrator places the audience in Joe Murray's bar, quickly explaining that he is Murray's "paid thug" (*TWAOP*, 199) whose ex-girlfriend, Greta, is now with Murray. After a night's sleep, drugs, a cold shower, and whiskey, the narrator assembles his sawn-off shotgun and Webley revolver and follows Murray's order to scare a man named Mitchell, the object of Murray's extortion. At the Mitchell estate, he is knocked down by the man who answers the door. In the house are Mitchell, his wife and child, who is about three or four years old, and two thugs, who threaten to break the narrator's legs. Seizing the moment, our speaker pulls his Webley and starts firing, hitting the man close to him. The other man fatally wounds Mitchell, but his gun jams before he can shoot the narrator, who grabs the shotgun, kills the second man, and then hits Mitchell's wife to keep her quiet. Finally, he calls Joe Murray, who says he will send someone over.

Convinced that Murray's men will kill him, the narrator shoots one of them and escapes with a gagged and bound Mrs

Mitchell and her child in the Mitchells' car. As the three make their escape to the N4, he imagines taking Greta back from Murray. At a lay-by, he convinces Mrs Mitchell that he had nothing to do with her husband's death and is not out to hurt her. After he removes the gag and unties her hands, she says she did not know the men with her husband. Later in the journey, Mrs Mitchell cleans up and withdraws money from an ATM. He observes that she is remarkably calm for a woman whose husband has just been shot to death.

He steals a car so they can travel incognito to Sligo, where his friend, Jeff, will find them a place to hide. As they drive, they introduce themselves to each other so that if they meet a roadblock, they can pretend to be married. The child is a girl named Niamh. In Boyle, Jeff takes them to an impressive estate in County Leitrim, on the Shannon, which stimulates another reverie in which the narrator and Greta enjoy a similar countryside retreat. He dozes and awakens to Niamh's hand on his face. Later, at a picnic arranged by Jeff and his family, Mrs Mitchell admits that Patrick Mitchell is not the child's father. At first upset over her duplicity, the narrator eventually puts his arm around Mrs Mitchell. She says to call her Anna, not Mrs Mitchell, a title which she considers funny. They return to the others, where the baby falls asleep in his arms.

After Jeff and his family leave, Mrs Mitchell and he confide in each other. The narrator feels the impulse to tell her about Greta, but does not, saying to the audience that he did not know where to begin. They fall asleep but awaken in the night to the sound of breaking glass. As he goes to the door, he is hit over the head. He regains consciousness the next morning, finding himself handcuffed and naked, sitting on the floor. He struggles with Murray's henchmen, who punch and kick him, causing him to lose consciousness and dream of Greta and Mrs Mitchell. Doused with water, he awakens to Murray telling him that Greta knew where he would go, that they had taken care of Jeff, and that there was a fire. Murray indicates that Mrs Mitchell and the child were killed but adds that Greta asked that the narrator be spared and so he will be left to be arrested as an accessory. As he leaves, Murray threatens to kill him if he mentions Murray's name to the police.

At his arrest, the narrator confesses to a kidnapping but says he was only the driver, that he was double-crossed by the others. Mrs Mitchell and Niamh were never found. In prison, he strikes up a friendship with his cellmate, Tom, largely based around recounting their sexual adventures. The narrator eventually confides in him about Mrs Mitchell. But Tom is released and they lose touch. The narrator says his own company is not good enough for him anymore; he drinks too much and is a loner. The play ends with him remembering a near-encounter with Greta after he was released from prison.

Once again, as in *Rum and Vodka*, the story is driven by the rhythm of the narrator's language and the images he draws for the audience. For example, as he stops at the lay-by with the child and Mrs Mitchell, he returns to the car after being sick, observing:

> Mrs Mitchell's head was against the door and the kid had climbed up on the seat beside her. She had a little blue dress on and one of her shoes was off. Her hair was the same colour as her mother's but her face was chubbier. Mrs Mitchell was very thin. Her hands looked sore from the clothesline that tied them. Her tracksuit bottoms were half off and I could have seen anything I wanted, but it just made me feel sick. (*TWAOP*, 213)

Like his predecessor in *Rum and Vodka*, this speaker is out of control and, subsequently, the energy of the play is drawn from the assertion that he refuses "to constrain my personality. I believe that that can lead to problems" (200).

But the opening sentence of *The Good Thief*, "Let's begin with an incident", suggests that this play will begin where *Rum and Vodka* left off (*TWAOP*, 199). The previous indulgence in obscene words, charming voices, and outrageous stories will be held somewhat in check as the playwright travels deeper into "the ineffable [. . .] a consciousness beyond self", an ambiguous place where the narrator can feel "sad all of the time. But I'm not sure what I felt sad about" (Brantley, 2001: B1; *TWAOP*, 235). Even as the speaker's evasions, self-deceptions and uncertainties drive the story, he often takes a more confessional tone than the protagonist in *Rum and Vodka*, as when he recognises "I had been beating her up and I knew it was wrong" or admits "I hate people with skills who can do stuff" (199, 200). In his more reflective moments, he is attentive to, even troubled by, the moral implications of his story. After relating his "very bad manners" at not giving Murray advice about Greta, he observes, "Well. That's the incident I wanted to begin with. It's sort of funny, isn't it? Kind of sick as well. There's just something not quite right about it. Hard to put your finger on though" (202). Even without a clear sense of his own identity, this character's instinct for ethics reflects his creator's confidence that a humorous consideration of moral imperative can be the subject of theatre.

Central to this narrator's ruminations is the possible value of mutuality. At the lay-by, it occurs to him that "if we kept our heads and worked together we might live to tell the tale" (*TWAOP*, 214). A few moments later, as he relates their escape from Dublin on the N4, his anger betrays his own failed attempts to achieve equality in his relationship with women. He begins with a fantasy that Greta might be worrying about him, but immediately he indulges in a mental tirade: "Did she think I was a fucking idiot? Then I thought about Joe Murray putting it up her arse. I called her a fucking bitch and apologised to Mrs Mitchell. I hadn't meant her. I hadn't meant her at all" (216). Lacking the sense of fair play later achieved by Git in *I Went Down*, this speaker respects neither women's intentions nor the value of boundaries in human relationships. But, like many other McPherson characters, he wants relief from feelings of guilt and worthlessness. On the way to Boyle, a nearby house stimulates a fantasy in which living in such a place would bring him contentment: "I wanted to live there so I could pull in, sit by the fire and have a few drinks. Eat my dinner and go to bed and in bed, my pretty wife would tell me she wasn't my judge and I'd sleep and sleep and dream until the next thing I'd do, which would be an interesting thing. And no one would bother me" (222).

In his most intense daydreams, he imagines the need for connection, conscience and even spirituality. Despite being paralysed by his angry alienation, he continually fantasises about Greta, what she would be doing, whether she was thinking of him (*TWAOP*, 235). When he awakens from his beating and discovers the destruction of Murray, he "wondered whose fault this was", indicating his sensitivity to the value of responsibility, at least in some situations. Most surprisingly, when Murray calls Mrs Mitchell "flat-chest Mitchell", he empathises with her predicament, understands that she was abused, and even entertains a sense of the transcendent: "Maybe that dream I'd had of her when I was getting that kicking was her soul and she had met me while things were happening to her body. I still like to think that" (234). Though he judges himself at the end of the play as "no good" (238), he has discovered in his thoughts of others, especially Greta and his cellmate Tom, that he "wanted to make someone else happy. I wanted to be there when they needed me" (237).

Rum and Vodka ends with the narrator late at night sitting before his sleeping children, broken but incapable of healthy reflection. The story brings the audience on a ride to the end of a dark road, but the nature of that darkness, the issues involved in the dilemma, are not explored by either the speaker or the audience. Reflection and choices lie before him, but the play does not go there. *The Good Thief* takes the logical next step. The second narrator once again insists that this play is about "an incident", not self-reflection; "I'm not the issue here" he says in the first moments of the play (*TWAOP*, 199). Nevertheless, at the conclusion, despite himself, he confesses, "My own company wasn't good enough for me anymore" (237). As this line suggests, *The Good Thief* finally resonates with the ironies and ambiguities implied in the word "good". Is he good at being a thief but not good at human feelings and relationships? Or is he a failure at his profession while being dogged by a conscience which asks him to act responsibly, sometimes even heroically, in the interest of others and justice? Is "goodness" a matter of behaviour, morality or courage?

More revealing than the narrator in *Rum and Vodka*, this speaker leaves the audience mulling over the central McPherson dilemma of freedom versus responsibility. Memory and resonant imagery haunt this thief in ways impervious to the narrator in the earlier play:

> Sometimes when the clouds are low and I look out the window with one eye on the pillow I still think about Mrs Mitchell and Niamh and Jeff's family. And I think about Greta and the time I saw her last year. It was a filthy wet day and she got out of a big car with a man twice her age. I thought about walking up to her but I was trying to get out of the rain. (*TWAOP*, 238)

Despite his protests that the story is not about him, he cannot repress thoughts of his responsibilities and actions, moral considerations which seep into his imagination. And his memories of Greta betray his lost love, failed opportunities for peace. But bastard circumstance, in the figure of the rain, is too much for him. Though he won't go that far in his confession, the audience senses in a way unexplored in the earlier play that courageous choices in the name of love — the light of Jesus — were available. Sadly, he never thought himself worthy of that light, and so he was not responsible, not good enough, to connect with Greta.

In *Rum and Vodka* there was no possibility for love because of the irremediable disjunction between the domestic and nightlife, between narcissism and responsibility. Because of their essential isolation, the characters in that play inhabit a world of pure fantasy. *The Good Thief* takes a step beyond *Rum and Vodka* by imagining love as a source of attachment and peace. But paralysis takes over in the second play; the lack of social limits and the failure of personal courage derail the caring impulses. At least in *The Good Thief* there is a history of sharing and loving memory, even if it is intruded upon by fear and anxiety. The narrator has a vision of commitment and contentment, imagined as a domestic world without judgement. It is a place where freedom from suppression and guilt is not necessarily followed by licence, violence and self-destruction. Unfortunately, he lacks the resources to make his fantasies real.

This Lime Tree Bower

The previous two plays, despite all their physical and emotional ramblings, are driven by single unnamed narrators. With *This Lime Tree Bower*, Conor McPherson shifted to multiple speakers — three — all named and two of whom are brothers. While the obvious Irish source for such a dramatic trio is Brian Friel's *Faith Healer*, McPherson's play is not driven by the disparities among multiple narrators as is Friel's earlier work. Instead, *Lime Tree* is a shared story, presented as a group project among actors/characters who inhabit a limbo between the monologue and traditional theatrical performance. The narrators share a common history, but, unlike Friel's characters, McPherson's do not offer variant readings to be analysed, weighed, and pieced together by the audience. With almost no conflict presented in the act of telling, the spotlight is on the mischief in the story itself, a focus which *Lime Tree* shares with *Rum and Vodka* and *The Good Thief.*

This Lime Tree Bower was first performed at the Crypt Arts Centre, in Dublin, on 26 September 1995. It was a co-production of Íomhá Ildánach and Fly By Night. The set design was by John O'Brien and the author, with lighting by Paul Winters. Philip Gray produced the initial staging. McPherson directed. The players were Ian Cregg (Joe), Conor Mullen (Ray), and Niall Shanahan (Frank). When restaged at the Bush Theatre, London, on 3 July 1996, it had the same cast. That production also was directed by the playwright, with lighting by Paul Russell. It was produced in New York, at Primary Stages, in the summer of 1999, directed by Harris Yulin.

As the play begins, the three actors walk casually on stage to tell their story, in turns. The first is seventeen-year-old Joe, who worships Damien, a schoolmate who Joe describes as cooler than the other students. Joe then introduces, by way of the story, his brother Frank, who is five years older, works in the family chipper, and believes their father's problems began when the old man borrowed money for his wife's funeral from Simple Simon McCurdie, a councillor. Joe returns to his attraction to Damien, admitting his embarrassment while listening to Damien's sexual exploits. When Damien talks Joe into skipping school one morning, they meet two good-looking girls. Later, at Damien's house, Joe is disturbed by the intimacy between Damien and his mother. After returning home, Joe masturbates while fantasising about the two girls. He adds that his sister, Carmel, is getting ready to see Ray, whom he introduces as a lecturer in philosophy. Joe suggests Ray is either a bit thick or blind to be going out with Joe's sister.

Ray takes up the story by declaring that he woke up in bed with one of his students, whose name he cannot recall. In the morning, after he has more gin and tonics before class, the girl comes to his office. After drinking alone and with the student throughout the day, he goes to see Carmel at the family chipper. Ray then gives way to Frank, who adds that his father has been drinking a bit too much, but otherwise things are fine. Simple Simon comes into the chipper but doesn't pay. That is when Frank starts developing his plan, as he recalls. That night at the Reynolds bar, Frank tells a notorious gunman that he needs a gun.

Joe explains that Frank told him he was going to rob Simple Simon on Monday, but Joe thinks Frank is just drunk. Joe drifts off to sleep, thinking about seeing Damien on Monday. Ray then continues the story by saying that on Saturday he takes Carmel to the Great Southern Hotel in Galway. On Sunday, he drinks with Tony Reagan, his professor, requesting a question-and-answer session during the visit by Wolfgang Konigsberg, an internationally famous philosopher, so Ray can "have this guy on the ropes" (*TWAOP*, 160). At a subsequent staff meeting, the department decides not to have such a session and Ray feigns moral outrage to upset Reagan.

Frank jumps immediately into his intrigue, describing himself preparing for the hold-up and walking to Simon's booking place, where he forces everyone to lie on the floor. When Simple Simon tells him the money isn't worth his time, Frank sticks the gun between the man's legs, causing him to mess his pants. Frank then makes Simon open the safe and remove his trousers so that Frank has time to escape through the back yard and over a fence. Charlie, Simon's nephew, almost catches up with him when Ray miraculously pulls up in his car.

After the interval, Joe begins by saying he received a call from Damien that Sunday night (the day before the robbery), asking him to go to a rough disco called Shadows. While Damien picks up a drunken blonde girl, Joe drinks at the bar and observes the action around him. On the way back to the girl's house, Damien takes her into a graveyard. When Joe goes to check on them, he sees Damien raping the girl; distressed, Joe cycles home, where he is sick. He dreams that night of the girl in the graveyard, another girl named Deborah whom he fancies at school, and a mysterious woman wearing a red dress and no shoes who laughs at herself. Damien doesn't show up for school, and when Joe returns home after classes, he discovers Frank and Ray with a pile of money.

Ray continues the story: he convinces the others to keep a low profile. Back at his school, Ray is studying Konigsberg's theories on the death of language when Reagan arrives to tell him that there will, in fact, be a short question-and-answer session after the third lecture. On Thursday night, Ray drinks a lot of wine at the reception for Konigsberg and ends up with the student again; she gives him oral sex in the car on the way to her place, where they are discovered by another man. Ray escapes home and spends much of the night in a cold bath, waking just one hour before the lecture. At the auditorium, when he stands to ask his question, he vomits profusely and then covers himself by asking the professor if he has ever seen anything quite like that. He thanks Konigsberg politely and exits.

After Frank interjects that he never heard that incident before, Ray says he has been saving it. Then Frank resumes the story. He buries the gun and keeps £30,000 under his bed. He is nervous about the investigation and whether Joe is unhappy with him, but he and Joe hide the money in the attic. The three young men decide they need some time away, and spend £5,000 of the money on a luxury hotel in Cork. On returning, they find a police car outside the chipper. Expecting a grilling about the robbery, they are surprised when the sergeant asks Joe if he knows Sarah Comisky, the girl from the Shadows club. She accused Damien, but Damien said it was Joe who raped her. After Joe agrees to a blood test, the three of them stay up late drinking beer, Joe reminiscing about his mother. The test comes back negative and Damien is charged. Frank sets aside money for Joe's college and travels to Chicago, from where he will send back more money to pay off the father's loan. Ray's book on ethics comes out, but no one reads it, which Ray does not mind. Joe finishes the play by reflecting on his feelings about the events described.

This Lime Tree Bower, which McPherson says "came to me as a dream about two brothers lying in bed, just talking" (Carty, 2000a: 2), at first seems like the earlier monologues tripled. As in *Rum and Vodka* and *The Good Thief*, the actors speak to the audience with the distance appropriate for a monologue, telling their story chronologically, relying on images for clarity within a complicated storyline. The sincerity of Joe and Frank follows the earlier narrators in compulsively relating what they assume are accurate descriptions of factual events. But Ray is more disingenuous than the other two; he is not satisfied with the stage directions to merely "remain on stage throughout [. . .] aware of each other" (*TWAOP*, 134). At one point, he tries to explain the excitement of "coming to a new place" by directly asking the audience, "Do you know what I mean?" then following with the assumption "No?" and a final "Fine" (159). And Ray is the one who surprises Frank with the vomiting at the reception, which provokes Frank to interject, "I never heard that", followed by Ray's playful assurance that he's "been saving it" (185).

At these two points, *Lime Tree* betrays itself as self-conscious drama. No longer just a player in another comic Irish tale, Ray becomes an alter ego for McPherson himself, flirting with the beginning of accepted theatre. In the first instance, he entertains the idea of going avant-garde ("coming to a new place"), enlisting the observers in the dramatic action and inventing a participatory, democratic stage. But he retreats, making clear in the process that he could have deconstructed his drama and prefers not to. "There is something," McPherson is saying in his conversation with his art, "that is fictional, magical about the theatrical situation". In the second disjunction, Ray plays with the beginning of traditional performance, the impulse to make a well-made play. But McPherson, imagining the loss of mischief when conventions take over a scene, instead returns his play to the organic rhythms in the story itself. At that moment *This Lime Tree Bower* declares itself free of the masters of drama, whether Irish, English, or Greek. According to McPherson, his generation no longer uses traditional form innocently or reflexively. Inspired by the organic model, new Irish playwrights are free to write with or without theatrical precedents. Creative mischief is always an option.

Thematically, the domestic scene, repeatedly betrayed in *Rum and Vodka* and the fantasised object of *The Good Thief*, is actively present in *This Lime Tree Bower*. The family here offers the grounding that escaped the characters in the previous plays. Joe, his siblings, and their father remember their mother with affection; even in death, she is a source of strength and purpose for them. But the loving and protective home is not the primary focus of *Lime Tree*. Like the other two plays, it studies the nature of freedom and the inevitability of moral considerations. Against a background of violence, *Lime Tree* considers the various responses to violation, both real and imaginary. Is Frank's action necessary? Is it just and right? Does the family gain or lose by mischief which requires concealment and flight? How genderised is aggression? What do women really want? By pointedly refusing to answer the play's questions, McPherson asks his audience to reflect on the characters' actions and, by identification, to imagine their own choices . . . and morality.

Despite obvious changes in form and place, *This Lime Tree Bower* is continuous with the previous two plays as another McPherson meditation on guilt, rebellion and freedom. Ray, the most intellectually trained of the men, returns the audience to the morally grey area between carelessness and responsibility when he rationalises his affairs with students: "Carmel could never find out. Our lives were too separate.

Of course, this was something I could lose my job over. But it was just the state I was in I couldn't give a fuck" (*TWAOP*, 146). He knows the implications of his decisions, but his need to reduce guilt requires that he risk his job and a satisfying relationship. A bright and insightful young man, he prefers to indulge his perversity rather than imitate the "nobility" of a person like Carmel:

> She had that nobility some people have about them. This showed me what I was and I thought it was a good thing our souls don't have smells. Because mine would stink. But at the same time I was proud. I was getting away with it. (159)

The foil to Ray is Frank, who has a history of choosing responsibility towards others over his own needs. In his view, "People always blame something, don't they?" (*TWAOP*, 149). And so he is motivated early in the play, he thinks, by his desire "to do something for" his father rather than act out Ray's selfishness (163). But eventually, even a socially good person like Frank has to deal with the guilt that accompanies his violent, illegal acts. After he hides the money under the bed, he notices that Joe is depressed and worries that his brother's feelings might be "my fault". Subsequently he, too, must rationalise his rebellion, claiming that "sometimes you have to decide that principles will only fuck you up, because no one else is ever moral" (186). Ironically, he defends his father by betraying the high moral position claimed by that same father. As he confesses to the audience, his dad

> had done everything by the rules in his life and look what happened. He was left on his own and shagged by bastards like McCurdie. But he was right. That was the thing. Well I didn't want to be right anymore. That's a load of meaningless toss. (188)

In the play's final irony, Frank's new ethical position forces his separation from the family in whose name he took his courageous (and humorous) action.

Joe's dilemma begins with his awakening to erotic desire. Typical of early adolescence, his initial object is another male, his new friend Damien: "I was in love with Damien," he admits, "in a friendly way." It is a physical, not laddish or high-minded, loyalty that drives him. Joe wanted Damien "to myself", which leads him to question "if that's what love is" (*TWAOP*, 171). He knows he doesn't want to behave like the "animals" at the Shadows club; he has, he asserts, "quite a lot of principles" (172). And so he reacts to Damien's rape of Sarah with an unsettling ambivalence: "The horrible thing was that what I saw made me sick to my stomach, but at the same time it was really turning me on. And that upset me" (174). Finally, his father asks Joe to accept this disjunction between idealism and the instinct for self-preservation and assertion when he explains to his son, concerning Damien's betrayal, that "people would do anything to save their skin. He said he knew it was disappointing but that was the way it was" (192).

Women are special cases in Joe's mind, beginning with his mother. Initially he struggles with her loss in his dreams and his conscious life: "I didn't want to waste time getting upset. It wasn't my fault. I didn't talk about her and I didn't like thinking about her. It scared me. And that was all there was to it" (*TWAOP*, 168). He is in the grip of guilt, loss and death as much as any of the characters. But Damien's behaviour and the haunting images of his mother (the woman in red of his dreams) and Sarah force Joe to explore his emotional life. Ironically, his guilt over his paralysis during the attack and his sexual fantasies afterwards frees Joe to recover happier, less guilt-ridden memories of the time when "Dad was teaching me how to skim stones on the beach. And Mum was trying to do it and she couldn't. It was summer and she had a red dress on. Dad was slagging her and she was laughing at herself. And

I felt safe and the safe feeling stayed" (192). Although his reflections on desire and intimacy are not resolved by the end
of This Lime Tree Bower, the image of his gentle and laughing
mother has been superimposed on that of the lost, abused
Sarah. Love has become, for him at least, an active force
against violence.

Lime Tree traces the plot of a political fantasy in which
three narrators share a story of class revenge. Trapped in a
seemingly endless cycle of unrewarding work and economic
exploitation by racketeers, the family stumbles toward fits of
careless freedom and a spot of cash. But most of the words in
the plays, and the final ones, are given to Joe's search for a
healthier understanding of his would-be friend Damien. On the
surface, the personal issues are settled as cleanly as the political ones, though with less fantasy. A relieved and happy Joe
declares in the final lines that This Lime Tree Bower is about a
time when "things started off good, and just got better"
(TWAOP, 193). But typical of a McPherson play, the audience is
asked to reason beyond such simplicities. Within the trappings
of a political melodrama, Lime Tree studies an isolated teenage
boy using remembered love as a source of insight and courage.
In his final words — "I can still see the girl" (193) — he looks
for respectful ways to approach women in a world full of bogus
male pretences about sex and aggression.

St Nicholas

In the interview included in this book, Conor McPherson says
that giving titles to his work is often the most difficult part.
For example, he added a degree of legitimacy and resonance
to This Lime Tree Bower by referring to Coleridge's dramatic
monologue, a similar study in loneliness. With St Nicholas, the
titling problem was solved by resorting more to irony than
literary reference. The fourth-century saint, who through
Dutch influence on New York became popularised as Santa

Claus, has little in common with McPherson's narrator. Canonised for his piety and abstinence, St Nicholas, the Bishop of Myra, is revered in Russia and Greece for his chastity, especially in the company of woman, and for his protection of children. While the speaker in *St Nicholas* does sober up and recommit to his wife and family at the end of the play, his obsessive pursuit of an actress would in no way have been sanctioned by the saint (even as a protector of travellers!). And this narrator's Helen is neither the first from Troy nor Yeats' second, Maud Gonne. Christmas serves here only in its absence; *Dublin Carol* is still three years away.

Conor McPherson wrote *St Nicholas* as writer-in-residence at the Bush Theatre, London, where the play was first produced on 19 February 1997. McPherson directed Brian Cox in the initial performance. Lighting was by Paul Russell. The artistic director was Mike Bradwell. The production moved to New York, at Primary Stages, where it opened on 11 March 1998, with the same actor and director. The artistic director for those performances was Casey Childs, with Deborah Constantine as lighting designer.

Like two of the earlier plays, *St Nicholas* is in two acts, identified by McPherson as "parts". The stage is bare, and the play is performed as a monologue. The unnamed narrator, a theatre critic, opens by saying that before he met the vampires, he "Thought [he] knew everything", though he "had no real thoughts about things" and was often on the verge of panic (*TWAOP*, 80–81). Drinking more as he got older, he lived in a comfortable house in the best area of Dublin, with an overweight wife and two kids. But then a girl got him into trouble, an actress named Helen who danced in *Salome* at the Abbey. He met her by lying to the cast in a pub, declaring the play the best thing he had seen, though he had given it a mediocre review. Their darling for the rest of the evening, he drove Helen to her home in Donnybrook, where she kissed him goodnight. Obsessed, he decided to follow her to London, where the play had a two-week run.

In London, he thinks about his wife but is more concerned when Helen arrives at the theatre on the arm of Peter Hamilton, the director. He follows the company into a bar and to their house near Bromley in Kent. There, with many drinks in him, he finds the courage to ring the doorbell. While Helen is asleep, he drinks cheap scotch with some of the others, claiming that his editor revised the review and he resigned over the incident. Left to sleep on the couch, he wakes up early and, inspired by a pornographic magazine, approaches Helen's bed but loses his nerve when he thinks of his own daughter. He flees to the ruins of the Crystal Palace. As night falls, he spies what appears to be a dog but then is revealed to be a young man. As they walk toward the city, the man introduces himself as William. They shake hands, and the critic feels comfortable, even imagining the man touching his face. Not what you'd expect from a vampire, he observes. The first "part" ends.

The vampire's lair is a decadent, shabby house on a wide suburban street, where he lives with five women, who recruit the critic for their nightly seductions by making him "want what they want" (*TWAOP*, 105). The next evening, William escorts him to a pub in Leicester Square, where the narrator meets Dominique, an attractive young woman who is celebrating her birthday. He uses his new charm to entice Dominique and her Oxford friends back to the vampire house. But he becomes sated with the carousing, considering it "just another one of the things that goes on. Nothing special" (114). Over the next few days, the critic avoids the beautiful vampires, talking only to William, who eventually bores him with advice on literary criticism, including advocacy of art for itself.

William then becomes a storyteller, describing a woodsman who rescues an old man and is rewarded with a watch which manipulates time. When the woodsman's wife dies, he uses the timepiece to return to her girlhood. Unfortunately, the watch breaks, leaving him stuck in the past, an old man with an unhappy child and pursued by the townspeople as a molester. Since William has no idea of the meaning of the story, the narrator concludes that vampires lack, and regret lacking, a conscience. He calls William an "unreflective animal" (*TWAOP*, 120) and consoles himself that he at least understands "the immorality" (121) of his actions over the past few years. Inspired by this insight, he smashes a jar of rice, the grains of which William compulsively needs to count, and declares this night of debauchery his last. But in Soho, he finds Helen and, once again tempted, leads her back to William's place. In the orgy that follows, he loses Helen in the crowd, only to discover her partially clothed on his bed and bitten by William. He rescues Helen, kisses her, and leaves her on the couch with one of her friends.

Feeling confident that he will begin talking to his wife and taking care of his children and health, the narrator declares "I had a story" (*TWAOP*, 129), implying that the telling of it has given "the chaos of [his] life form and shading" (Brantley, 1998: par. 12). As the play ends, he turns to the audience and reflects that love at first sight is too trusting, while gradual love lacks deep passion. If you avoid these extremes, he says, your presence "blesses everyone else here [. . .] Because you're the embodiment of hope [. . .] hope incarnate." He finishes by asking the audience: "Where are you? Where are you? Where?" (130). Taking one step further than Ray in *This Lime Tree Bower*, in the final seconds of *St Nicholas*, the critic/narrator breaks down the final illusion — of the monologue itself — in service of what McPherson identifies in the interview in this book as Aristotelian moderation. Unconnected with the narrative of the play, this love of a divine mean is offered as a purely rational, untheatrical choice which is left irritatingly, intrusively in the ears of the audience. It is, in fact, McPherson's own.

Even more than earlier narrators, this one is explicitly frustrated by his inability to integrate his physicality and morality. On the one hand, he says his obsession with Helen is an expression of his "very Nazi" approach to life, his belief that being "the physical specimen you always wanted to be" would give people confidence and "we could all concentrate on just being nice to each other" (*TWAOP*, 91–92). But at the same time, he says it is not primarily a sexual attraction: "If she were ever to give herself to me, it'd be her acceptance of me", in his mind, that would lead to a happy domestic situation (91). Unable to reconcile these impulses, he lives in a paralytic limbo: "I couldn't move. Reason had crept into the room behind me and caressed my neck. This girl. I could only crave her attention, and ruin her" (101). Desire is equated, in his mind, with destruction. And reason seems more erotic than sexual attraction. Guilt and confusion are in the saddle and ride his emotional life.

What he loses in the ability to act he gains in intellectual focus. He is quite glib, for example, about vampires, telling the audience: "They appeal to the older part of us. What we share with the animals" (*TWAOP*, 105). More educated and verbally gifted than earlier narrators, this man even knows about the seductive nature of authoritarianism in such troubled, incoherent times: "It's easy, when you're told what to do. When the choices narrow. When you're under authority. That's why there's so many madcap schemes and bad artists" (112). Like his author talking about George W. Bush in the interview in this book (see page 147), the speaker in *St Nicholas* senses the value in knowing that you don't know. He is just as clear about the pointlessness of dehumanised art. Following the lead of the Coleridge poem, which declares at the beginning of *Lime Tree*, "No sound is dissonant which tells of life" (133), this critic/narrator associates vampirism with "art [. . .] for itself", which lacks the reflection, choice, and reason which help mankind rise above the natural will to survive (116, 120,

121, 127). As he shares with the audience his journey from the controlled world of critical judgement into the chaos of personal obsession, he follows Conor McPherson's path of reasonable mischief toward a defence of self-reflection and personal responsibility.

Like the playwright gaining confidence in his artistic impulses, this narrator can even stop the progression of his story to remind his audience of the assumptions and rules of their time together. If the people before him are becoming uncomfortable with the images and violence suggested by his words, he explains:

> I have the freedom to tell you this unhindered, while you can sit there assured that no one is going to get hurt. Possibly offended, but you'll live. We're all quite safe here. Safe to say things like, "If they were vampires, why don't their victims become vampires?" (*TWAOP*, 108)

If the observers before him seem a bit lethargic, he attributes it to the consumerism which makes them sleepy; anticipating his author's views on Hollywood films, the narrator declares his audiences should be wary of "relying on the lazy notions foisted upon you by others in the effort to make you buy more popcorn" (108). Also like his creator, he wants to engage his audience by reminding them that we all live in a state of confusion which fosters destructive judgements: "So don't sit there and cast judgement on the credibility of what I say, when you don't even know why you aren't floating off your seats" (109).

St Nicholas began as a dream, McPherson has explained, in which the writer was "procuring people for a house of vampires, and there was this pretty girl and she'd been bitten and I gave her paracetamol and the play got stuck in my head then" (Wolf, 1998a: AR8). Following the lead of "the epic stories of the old Gaelic tradition", the writer transformed his dream into "a contemplation of narrative itself, exploring the extraordinary willingness of an audience to be led step by step from the familiar to the outrageous [. . .] in this case, moving from the humdrum life of a bitter Dublin theatre critic to a weird encounter with vampires" (O'Toole, 1998: 19). But *St Nicholas* is partially deconstructed theatre, not a specimen from the oral tradition. As McPherson reminds his interpreters, it "plays with the idea of being in a theatre with a theatre critic who is really an actor pretending to be a theatre critic being judged by theatre critics. All those levels of perception: it's so theatrical" (Wolf, 1998a: AR8). The "magic" of storytelling appears in *St Nicholas* primarily as playful decoration; its mischief focuses on the stifling of integrated, passionate writing by cerebral, deadly anger. An outrageous joyride, *St Nicholas* also is an essay on aesthetics and a playful study of the moral dilemmas which surface when erotic attachment fails to grow into love, when ecstasy must decide between transcendence and self-annihilation.

Integral to Conor McPherson's achievement in these early plays is his experimentation with the monologue. Historically, the form is often linked to the soliloquy, the convention in which an actor speaks directly to the audience, offering the thoughts of the character he or she is playing. Although offered in a kind of trance, the traditional soliloquy seems mostly rational and rhetorically sound. Like the aside, it is a truthful source of information, even when filtered through the character's consciousness. When similar speeches borrow from the speaker's unconscious, they are usually defined as interior monologues. Technically, then, the dramatic monologue is a special case, a literary rather than theatrical one, characterised by the presence of a dramatic situation involving a recognisable but silent listener. Such a context allows, and in most cases requires, the reader to form impressions and judgements different from the narrator's. The agendas of the speaker in the situation described become the central focus of the work, not the beauty or reliability of what is said.

McPherson's use of these conventions of the dramatic monologue distinguishes his plays from those which employ the traditional monodrama, aside or soliloquy, for example. The title *This Lime Tree Bower* is the clearest indicator of this borrowing. The specific reference is the poem "This Lime Tree Bower My Prison", by Samuel Taylor Coleridge, in which the poet converses with Charles Lamb, his house guest, who walks through the English countryside as the poet remains behind, immobilised by an injury. That speaker hopes that the city boy Lamb will feel the nurturing presence of nature, partly for Lamb's own peace of mind but also because host and guest will be connected through their common and simultaneous appreciation of the beauty around them. It is a poem about loneliness mollified by friendship, nature, and art. Wordsworth's "Tintern Abbey" and "Ruined Cottage" and Coleridge's "Frost at Midnight" have similar dramatic situations and prescriptions. In the Victorian period, Robert Browning, of course, added psychological and social pathology to the dramatic monologue in poems like "Porphyria's Lover" and "My Last Duchess".

In modern Irish theatre, monologues have been familiar exercises for writing and acting. But it was Brian Friel's 1979 play *Faith Healer* that gave the form an unprecedented complexity and respectability. That play describes the relationships among a faith healer, Frank Hardy, his manager Teddy, and Frank's lover/wife Grace. Like McPherson's, Friel's characters recognise the presence of the audience. But *Faith Healer* emphasises the differing versions of the shared history and allows these characters to use a public rhetoric. They are rational and explanatory. Friel's 1994 play *Molly Sweeney* is closer to a McPherson play. Like *Faith Healer*, the second play is not a single monologue. As in *Faith Healer*, three characters — Molly Sweeney (a woman blind from early childhood), her husband

Frank, and Mr Rice, the physician who temporarily restores her sight — describe Molly's operation to cure her disability. Although not particularly influential on McPherson's early monologues, this play anticipates *This Lime Tree Bower*'s use of multiple narratives to tell a common story. In both cases, it is the story that is the subject, rather than the conflicts and disparities between the speakers.

Even though *Molly Sweeney* and *This Lime Tree Bower* are structurally similar, the plays demonstrate the essential differences between Friel and McPherson. As in *Faith Healer*, Friel respects the conventions and dignities of public talk in *Molly Sweeney*. It is essay-like in its emphasis on clarity and reasoned expression. On the other hand, even McPherson's most reasonable characters are one step from an emetic, compulsive barrage saturated with hidden agendas and prevarication. And they don't just recall a story. They use their engaged, active imaginations to recreate it alluringly before the audience. As the play develops, the locus of the drama shifts from the story to the captive audience, who become "the hidden character [. . .] to whom the story is told", a role requiring spectators, and actor, to be "doubly willing to share the sacred space" of the theatre (Cox, 1999: par. 8, 17). Despite all the emphasis in McPherson's work on trusting the stories of charming bastards, the dilemmas faced by the characters remain after all the pyrotechnics in the telling. The writer expects the audience to respond with a degree of reason and judgement claimed by the narrators but never fully realised in their performances.

It is not enough to say that Conor McPherson expresses the natural affinity between the Irish storytelling tradition and the literature of subjectivity. Each of his so-called monologues is distinctive and experimental. *Rum and Vodka* employs an emotionally insulated narrator whose story relies on an exhausting sense of physical action. The narrator in *The Good Thief* is more troubled and less explosive in his description, despite the excessive violence in his tale. *St Nicholas* is more aware of itself as a physical and emotional journey, as well as an exploration of conscience and even aesthetics. Only with *This Lime Tree Bower* does Conor McPherson seem close to Brian Friel in the use of overlapping storylines and families in crisis. Even then, McPherson keeps the issue somewhat hidden from the characters' consciousness. Typically, the younger writer deemphasises the contradictions among his multiple narratives. So far, he has explored those potentialities of the monologue less in his own work than in his direction of, for example, Eugene O'Brien's *Eden*.

Chapter Three

The Weir:
The Play and Its Reputation

The Weir was commissioned by the Royal Theatre. It was written in Leicester, England, while McPherson was sharing a rental house with his girlfriend at the time, Ríonach ní Néill. The play is set in a specific Irish locale, Jamestown on the River Shannon, and is based on

> visits to Leitrim to see my granddad. He lived on his own on a country road in a small house beside the Shannon. I remember him telling me once that it was very important to have the radio on because it gave him the illusion of company. We'd have a drink and sit by the fire. And he'd tell me stories. When you're lying in bed in the pitch black silence of the Irish countryside it's easy for the imagination to run riot. (McPherson, 1997b: Preface, *viii*; also quoted in Renner, 1998: 63)

From such memories of impressionable times in rural Ireland listening to his grandfather against a background of silence, darkness and isolation, the writer fashioned his most success- ful play about the personal and ethical rewards of storytelling.

The Weir was first performed at the Royal Court Theatre Upstairs, London, on 4 July 1997, where it played until mov-

ing on 18 February 1998 to the Royal Court Theatre Downstairs. The production was directed by Ian Rickson, designed
by Rae Smith, with lighting by Paule Constable. The players
were Jim Norton (Jack), Brendan Coyle (Brendan), Kieran
Ahern (Jim), Gerard Horan (Finbar for the Upstairs production), Des McAleer (Finbar, Downstairs) and Julia Ford (Valerie). The production which opened in July of 1998 at the
Gate Theatre in Dublin had the same director and set designer, with Norton, Coyle and Ahern reprising their respec-
tive roles. Dermot Crowley played Finbar, and Hilary
Reynolds was Valerie. It was premiered in the United States
on 1 April 1999, at the Walter Kerr Theatre, again directed
by Ian Rickson. The producers were Thomas Viertel, Richard
Frankel, Steven Baruch, Marc Routh, Jujamcyn Theatres,
Manhattan Theatre Club, and the Turnstyle/Ambassador
Theatre Group. For the American production, Finbar was
played by Dermot Crowley and Valerie by Michelle Fairley.
Again, Rae Smith and Paule Constable were responsible for
design and lighting. Sound was by Paul Arditti and the stage
manager was Brian Meister.

As defined by McPherson, *The Weir* is an ensemble play,
which opens with Jack entering a rural bar attached to a farm-
house, having trouble with the tap, and opening a bottle of
beer. Brendan, the proprietor, enters and tidies up at the bar
while they discuss the weather, a visit by Brendan's sisters,
and Jack's improved luck at betting. Jack mentions that Finbar
Mack has been bragging that he sold or rented Maura
Nealon's house to a single woman, from Dublin, whom he
has been escorting around town, despite his married state,
and plans to bring her by the pub to meet "the natives"
(*TWAOP*, 10). They agree that Finbar is just showing off in
front of the single men, "a juvenile carry on", as Jack calls it
(11). They reassure each other that freedom, not marriage, is
the better way. When Jimmy enters, they continue the small
talk, including Finbar's intentions and the arrival of the tour-

ists, called "the Germans". As they light cigarettes, Finbar
arrives with Valerie, the woman who has taken the Nealon
house. The men begin to tell her the history of the place, including the story of the fairy road, which they ask Jack to tell,
forgetting that it is about the house where Valerie is to live.

Jack tells of the night in 1910 or 1911, when Maura's
mother, Bridie, heard knocking at the front door and then at
the back, at first believing someone was playing a joke on her
mother, who was herself a trickster. A priest blessed the
doors and the windows, after which the knocking stopped,
except for once later when the weir was being built. The
house was supposedly constructed on a fairy road between a
fort at the top of Brendan's property and a pebble beach in
the cove. At the conclusion of his tale, Jack adds that Finbar
had his own run-in with the fairies. Finbar continues the storytelling by describing the Walsh family, who, when Finbar
was a young man, moved into the old Finnerty house. Their
youngest daughter, Niamh, was experimenting with a ouija
board, which released a spirit she subsequently saw on the
stairs. The doctor gave her a sedative and Father Donal said
it was only her imagination. Then a brother called from Long-
ford, reporting that everyone was upset because an old
woman who used to take care of Niamh and the other children had fallen down a staircase to her death. That night,
while smoking, Finbar felt the presence of someone on the
stairs and has never had a cigarette since.

Jim next tells of what happened to him twenty years before when he and Declan were asked by a priest to dig a shallow grave in the rain. They drank poitín as they worked and
were amazed when the hearse arrived with only two or three
attendants. While Jim waited for Declan to get a tarpaulin, a
man approached to say they were at the wrong grave. Tired
and sick, Jim followed the man to another grave, that of a
young girl. The man touched the gravestone and finally left to
return to the church. At home that night, Jim's fever broke,

but his mother would not let him go to the service. Later, she brought him the paper; in the obituaries, he saw a picture of the man he met, identified as the man whose grave they had dug. One night, much later, Declan told him that the dead man had a reputation for perversion, which explained why he wanted to visit the little girl's grave.

While Valerie visits the ladies' room, Jack and Finbar argue over the inappropriateness of the stories told by Finbar and Jim. Finbar apologises to Jim and Jack for the story he told, but insists he has no designs on Valerie. Jim and Finbar shake hands and have a drink. When Valerie returns, the others say they will put an end to the stories. But Valerie demurs, saying that hearing them reminded her that she's "not . . . bananas" (*TWAOP*, 53). And she begins her story. She and her husband, Daniel, had a daughter, Niamh, who at five years of age enrolled in a swimming class at the Central Remedial Clinic in Clontarf. Niamh enjoyed swimming but was very afraid of the dark at night, imagining people coming up the stairs and knocking in the walls. In March, Valerie arrived late to pick up her daughter from a sponsored swim at the CRC, only to learn that Niamh had hit her head in the pool and could not be resuscitated. Afterwards, Daniel threw himself into work while Valerie felt lost and alone. Then, one morning when Valerie was home by herself, she answered the phone and heard Niamh asking her to come pick her up at Nana's. The child said she heard children knocking in the walls and saw a man getting ready to cross the road towards her. Daniel responded by saying she imagined the call, but Valerie wanted him to accept her feeling that the child was out there, still needing her mother.

The men start arguing among themselves about what happened and what she could or should do. But Valerie tells them to stop fighting, that their opinions are comforting because they show she is not crazy. Finally, they put the argument aside and say how sorry they are about her daughter.

As Jim and Finbar prepare to leave, Finbar says he will check on her in a day or two and kisses her awkwardly on the cheek. The three remaining people move closer to the stove, share more drinks, and contemplate how hard it will be for Jim when his mother dies. Brendan gives Valerie a large brandy, and the men raise their glasses to her. Valerie asks if Jack has children, and he says he never married but offers his story of the girl he courted from 1963 to 1966. When she moved to Dublin, he stayed home and became estranged from her. Eventually, she was to marry another, and Jack decided to attend the ceremony in Phibsboro, grinning as he caught his ex's eye during the service. Afterwards, he skipped the reception to hang out in a small, dark pub, where he watched as the barman made him a sandwich, a kindness which brought tears to his eyes. Humbled, he returned to the reception. He adds to his story the observation that he hasn't felt such proper humility since that night.

Jack prepares to leave, adding that at least his wasn't a ghost story and "We'll all be ghosts soon enough" (*TWAOP*, 67). Brendan offers Jack a lift, Valerie wants to help Brendan clear the glasses, and Jack holds Valerie's coat for her as she prepares to leave. They gossip briefly about the absent others and then agree that all the men will be back, even when the Germans arrive, if Valerie returns, which she says she will. As they discuss where the people they call the Germans are really from, Valerie finds Brendan's keys. They walk to the door, and Brendan turns off the light.

Conor McPherson's visits to his grandfather's home, where the writer heard many ghost stories, were clearly the genesis of *The Weir*. But when the writer composed his play, he did not offer these stories in isolation, as examples of the spooky or uncanny. At the very least, they reflect an undercurrent of self-revelation and hidden motives. As Benedict Nightingale has observed: "The tales [. . .] are confessions, or unintended revelations of the narrator's psyche, or attempts to impress and dominate, or ways of facing painful truths, or some combination of those things" (1998b: AR8). As McPherson sees it, the weir is a metaphor for the pub as a place of revelation for the storytellers; the weir "On one side [. . .] is quite calm, and on the other side water is being squeezed through. Metaphorically, the play is about a breakthrough. Lots under the surface is coming out." While sharing their stories, the characters "are reminded of their situation in life, of who they are, and they either face up to it or they don't" (Gussow, 1999: B1, 3).

But the play is also about relationships, not just hidden impulses and motives. As self-serving as their stories are intended to be, the men eventually give solace to each other and, more importantly, to Valerie. Once she becomes sensitive to their stories and the dramas they imply, Valerie is, as her author explains,

> kind of compelled to tell her story because of the way the evening is progressing. She needs to tell it. The play is a very simple idea really; someone needs some support and consolation, and she finds a place where she gets it. (Renner, 1998: 21)

The power of *The Weir* is generated by the accumulation of empathy and care among the group as the stories are told, interpreted, and responded to; it is not a forum for singular tales: "Each of the stories [. . .] deepens and expand[s] the others" into a unified study of "how people comfort and distract one another in the midst of desolation and grief" (Brantley, 1999a: B26; Renner, 1998: 21). The stories are redemptive acts of connection against the profound sense of loneliness which pervades McPherson's plays:

> the subject isn't just things that go bump in the night, but the loss and loneliness that eventually haunt every life. [. . .] Though a feeling of individual isolation in a

baffling and often hostile world pervades *The Weir*, the stories woven by its characters become solid, if temporary, bridges among them. And if the disturbing mysteries of existence haven't been given explanations, they have been given forms, and that in itself is a victory. (Brantley, 1999a: B1, 26; also quoted in Cummings, 2000: 311)

By the end of the play, the empathy and kindness that is established among the characters in *The Weir* gain religious resonance. Jim, for example, reassures Valerie by asserting the sacredness of the child's life and his personal need to worship her innocence; he declares, "I'm very sorry about what's happened to you. And I'm sure your girl is quite safe and comfortable wherever she is, and I'm going to say a little prayer for her, but I'm sure she doesn't need it. She's a saint" (*TWAOP*, 60–61). Valerie's presence is equally comforting to the other men; as Jack Kroll explains, once the men are able to focus on her needs, their "fairies and demons and spirits are instantly humanised, as if the woman has conjured up the ghost that lies in wait for everyone who inevitably suffers" (1999: 77). In the face of the essential loneliness of the human condition, the smallest act of comfort can gain the import of the most sacred communion, as Jack learns in the bar after the wedding of the woman he loved:

> And I took this sandwich up and I could hardly swallow it, because of the lump in my throat. But I ate it all down because someone I didn't know had done this for me. Such a small thing. But a huge thing in my condition. It fortified me, like no meal I ever had in my life. And I went to the reception. And I was properly ashamed of myself. (*TWAOP*, 66–67)

Beneath all the banter and intrigue, the subject of *The Weir* is, finally, "intimacy, the unspoken, sacred feeling that binds old friends and can flow suddenly between new ones" (Isherwood, 1999: 154).

In addition to religious images and values, *The Weir* also reprises the concern for morality that informed McPherson's earlier monologues. Although these characters are neither as perverse nor as self-destructive as the earlier speakers, they consider, as their predecessors did, the value of repression in human communities. Storytelling itself, Jack notes, needs to be restrained in the interest of Valerie's need for peace: "Ghosts and angels and all this? Fuck them. I won't have it. Because I won't see someone like you being upset by it. You've enough to . . . deal with, for fuck's sake" (*TWAOP*, 68). In this spirit, the title suggests the benefits of inhibiting the natural flow of emotion and behaviour, including sexuality. When Finbar notes that the weir in the picture on the wall "is to regulate the water for generating power for the area and for Carrick as well" (27), he anticipates Jack's recognising that "You should only catch someone's eye for the right reason" (67). Or, to return to the metaphor, the restraining of their natural impulses makes possible a more reasonable form of energy, one which serves the order of loving relationships.

Before the play was staged, McPherson returned to the place that had inspired *The Weir*, this time accompanied by the director, Ian Rickson, and set designer, Rae Smith. For the most part, his memories were similar to those which served the writing experience:

> I remembered sitting with my granddad, Jack, in his little house outside Jamestown where he lived alone. Smoking, tipping ash into the fire, drinking bottled stout from a six-pack. And a world, half imagined, half rooted in reality, just about visible to me in the dark. A world of lost afternoons in suburban and rural bars. Of closing your eyes in the dim light. (*TWAOP*, 306)

But he adds a note absent from descriptions of the genesis of the play. The writer explains that in those times of floating unreality, he felt part of "a community who couldn't or wouldn't judge you" (306). Tracing the line of McPherson's personal history, *The Weir* evolved from remembrances of family storytelling into a vision of a world beyond isolation and guilt. It is a theatrical moment which imagines judgement and mischief replaced by "consolation for loss, loneliness, and regret" (Cummings, 2000: 308).

The success of *The Weir* was made possible by Conor McPherson's creative partnership with the London theatre community over the previous year. The initial catalyst was The Bush Theatre, which brought *This Lime Tree Bower* from Ireland to the larger English stage and then supported the creation of *St Nicholas* with a writer-in-residency. Between July 1996, when *Lime Tree* premiered at the Bush, until July 1997, the opening of *The Weir*, McPherson's work received very positive reviews, which brought him fame in both England and Ireland. But there was relatively little to prepare the young playwright for the reputation of *The Weir*, first at the Royal Court Theatre in London, at the Gate in Dublin, and then at the Walter Kerr in New York City. By the end of 1999, McPherson had added the *Evening Standard* Award and the London Critics Circle Award, as well as the Olivier BBC Award, to his list of accomplishments. More importantly for a playwright who obsessively explores the nature of drama and the theatrical, he gained the financial security and reputation which would allow him to "sit down [. . .] and write a play for nobody" (White, 2000: par. 3). Meanwhile, McPherson was unaware that, back in Ireland, he had been discovered by the movie people.

Chapter Four

The Playwright as Filmmaker

I Went Down

Without his knowledge, Conor McPherson's participation in filmmaking began in 1994. Robert Walpole, the producer, and Paddy Breathnach, the director, saw the playwright's *The Good Thief* in the Dublin Theatre Festival during October of that year. As Breathnach explained in an interview for *Film Ireland*, "we both really liked it but very quickly afterward we got involved in *WRH* [*Waterford Regional Hospital*, a documentary]. So we said 'we must link up with this guy, he's really good', but we didn't do it for quite a while, until we'd finished shooting *WRH*" (Walpole and Breathnach, 1997: 12). It was not until May of 1995 that Walpole had the time to call and arrange a meeting of the three at the Irish Film Centre. The writer's first impression was that the others were "a team": "Paddy does the talking. Rob hangs back a little. Supportive. They're practised. They're grown-ups. Paddy is tall, very dark. Considered. I think he's foreign. Rob is shorter, fairer, eager to laugh" (*IWD, v*). After directing *Ailsa*, a study of obsession photographed in a consciously European style, Breathnach wanted to pursue a more commercial project. He handed McPherson "some photocopied stories, ancient Irish myths", including the revenge story *The Sons of Tuireann*. Walpole

wrote "a cheque for a hundred quid" for start-up on a different kind of film, "something modern, urban. Irish but universal" (*vi*), "a story about territory" (Walpole and Breathnach,
1997: 13).

But this first attempt went nowhere. The story did not
click with McPherson: "I read it and I think it's stupid. People
casting spells and turning their enemies into goats and so
forth. I don't understand what Paddy wants." Luckily, however, the writer agreed to another meeting in which he
shared his confusion about the story and expectations, saying,
as he remembers it, "I don't understand what the hell this is
about." At that crucial moment, humour magically descended
into the ensuing silence, rescuing the chance for a film:
"Paddy frowns. He's not sure either. Rob laughs at Paddy.
Paddy laughs at himself. We forget about the myths and I can
see I'm going to get on well with this pair" (*IWD, vi*). They
decided to keep the contemporary story about "revenge and
the double cross" but drop everything else (Walpole and
Breathnach, 1997: 13).

I Went Down was collaborative from the beginning of the
project. Together they decided to avoid "the North" or drug-
dealing, which they considered a too-obvious setting for an off-
beat film about Irish gangsters. McPherson even wrote treat-
ments "about losers" for Walpole, but no one offered money.
The writer, as he now admits, even began to feel that such
work was "pointless if no one's going to respond". The project
was temporarily stalemated. But McPherson eventually recov-
ered his resilience, despite the lack of up-front money, and decided in June of 1995 to write the script anyway. As he
describes it, "I decide I don't need any money. I'm on the dole
and I'm writing the first draft." By the next month, July,
McPherson had written "ten or fifteen pages" (*IWD, vi*).

The three men met at Treasure Films on Eustace Street
and retired to the roof, where the writer acted out his
thriller for them, a story which included many characters who

will survive into the final product. The producer and director loved what they saw, but not in the way the now-screenwriter expected:

> Paddy and Rob are laughing out loud. I'm a bit thrown. I think it's supposed to be ugly and terrifying. But the characters are *so* concerned with being tough or threatening that their demonstrative natures can't help but reveal their insecurities beneath the surface. There's so much stupid posturing, they verge on being clown-like. (*IWD*, *vi*)

The artists have found their niche, a film which plays with the thriller genre but has a unique "mixture of suspense and slap-stick" (*vi*).

McPherson became re-energised. Over the following days and weeks he continued writing, checking in with Rob and Paddy, acting out the story on the roof at Treasure Films. He gained further time and focus in September when he joined his girlfriend in Leicester. Writing regularly now, he completed 60 pages. But once again things went off track. Breathnach was not totally happy with the direction it was taking. It was too dark and violent and had lost the humour which the director viewed as essential. Losing confidence, McPherson nevertheless finished the first draft, which he considered "rushed and patchy". They tried once again for development money, but there were still no takers in September (*IWD*, *vi–vii*).

By Christmas of 1995, McPherson began a new draft, following Breathnach's advice "to move it, to spread it [. . .] let them go on a journey, a quest" (Walpole and Breathnach, 1997: 13). This time, he kept it lighter through thirty pages. Feeling that he had embarrassed himself by talking too freely to a journalist at the Irish Film Ball at Ardmore Studio, the writer called Walpole to apologise. But he was not chastised. Instead, the producer gave him reassurance that the second draft is "great" and the film would get made. Encouraged, he continued the writing, finishing the revised screenplay in the spring of 1996. They sent it out. But still no money was offered. McPherson decided: "I need to do something radical. I decide to move into Paddy and Rob's office" (*IWD*, *vii*).

This set-up worked, despite the constant interruptions and noise as Walpole and Breathnach worked on their documentary films *The Road to America*, *The Charlton Years*, and *Waterford Regional Hospital*. The collaborators' insistence that the young writer move the story outside Dublin, take it away from familiar North Dublin neighbourhoods and characters in pursuit of an open-ended journey, finally paid off (*IWD*, 114). Things fell into place. In McPherson's words:

> The phone is ringing. Couriers are coming in and out. I'm chasing the comedy and slimming down the plot. We're out of Dublin. The task is simple. It keeps getting more complicated. I'm testing gags out on whoever's in the office. I try bits of dialogue. It's taking shape. We discuss various endings. We decide on one. I write it and we go to the pub. I want to call it *I Went Down*. They send the script out. Within days the phone is ringing. (*vii*)

After repeated tries, they finally had the money.

In the collaborative process of making *I Went Down*, Breathnach and Walpole often took the lead. As they say in "Genre, Pace and Landscape", the interview included as an appendix in the published shooting script, the director and producer were attracted to the "freshness, rawness and naturalness" in the writer's work, but they felt the need to shape it for the needs of genre and film narrative (*IWD*, 114). By requiring a trip beyond Dublin, they would, in Walpole's words, create "a world that was interesting to people outside Ireland". Such an opening up, "a wider journey where Git and Bunny just aren't comfortable anywhere", paid dividends in characterisation as well. The general disorientation of the characters created more sympathy for the protagonists; their predicament could be identified with more readily by the audience. The consequence was a finished film with more "heart" (115).

The filmmakers, as Breathnach explains, were reacting to "Hood" movies, feeling that their film needed to find a unique place within the well-developed genre. By "making it expansive", getting out of a single locale and establishing a journey, they were adding "an element of quest" which necessarily changed the characters. The most dramatic change was in Bunny (in earlier drafts named Jimmy) who, as Robert Walpole describes, is changed from a "real headbanger [. . .] a hard, gross kind of unattractive character who wandered around the house in stained tracksuits, hitting his kids" into "the more fumbling, big-hearted but no less explosive or aggressive Bunny Kelly" (*IWD*, 113). The filmmakers also, as Paddy Breathnach notes, wanted to avoid the history of Irish films which portrayed "the guilt-ridden nation, the IRA storylines, people who are always pissed out of their heads, horses, [and the idea that you] couldn't have sex with someone from your own country and enjoy it" (113).

As the director says in the conversation published in the book *I Went Down*, much fine writing and powerful acting needed to be trimmed in editing because in the film the "hunger is for the payoffs from the stuff we've established. We have to push on and let people know what's going to happen with these things." The establishing of a "rhythm" or "pace" made some of McPherson's personal ideas and work on individual scenes expendable (*IWD*, 118). The tendency for the writer's characters to tell their stories and explain away their versions of what's happened and who they are had to be sacrificed, in Paddy Breathnach's view, to the realities of a variant genre, the Irish thriller. There is, he discovered while making *I Went Down*, a relationship between genre and landscape. Say if the chase was happening in the desert in Arizona — and they stop to make a phone call — the sense of greater distance is going to have an impact. You can use that feeling of space, the opportunities to pause are better. But when you're on those roads in rural Ireland, you don't have that sense of isolation to the same extent. (118–19)

They believed the aimlessness would be magnified by the indulgent dialogue and the more claustrophobic Irish landscape.

Such a cinematic environment, in Breathnach's view, would require McPherson to modify his instincts for dark theatrical humour:

The humour you can have in the theatre can sometimes be created out of tension. A live audience sharing an experience can be prompted to laugh at things they mightn't normally think of as funny. But in the cinema if you go down a dark road — you go down a dark road. Maybe in an American landscape — Tarantino can sometimes do it — something cruel can be funny. But I feel in this landscape I just wouldn't have been able to do that. (*IWD*, 115)

The film and characters were purposely humanised by demythologising the Irish countryside, creating a "landscape [. . .] resonant with the dirty deeds of contemporary urban humanity rather than heroic deeds of ancient history or the beauty of bountiful Nature" (McLoone, 1999: 30). The resulting sense of placelessness made *I Went Down*

a film of elsewheres. Apart from the opening and closing sequences the action is in all senses "beyond the pale": around a detached, semi-deserted house in the midlands somewhere, in a wood, on the road, in the petrol-station, the anonymous bars and motels.

> [. . .] We may be told that certain scenes are in Cork,
> but the city is unrecognisable. (Scallan, 1998: 24)

In the process, *I Went Down* joined *Donnie Brasco* and *Trojan Eddie* as baroque gangster films more dedicated to characters than intrigue.

I Went Down uses intertitles to describe the action and focus of each section of the film. The first of these is the opening lines of Plato's *Republic* — "I went down to the Pireaus yesterday with Glaucon, the son of Ariston" (*IWD*, 3) — followed by a brief prison scene. Sabrina, the ex-girlfriend of Git, comes to visit him, asking that he facilitate her relationship with Anto, Git's best friend, when Git is released in three months. She returns Git's ring. Upon release, Git goes to Tom French's pub, where Sabrina reminds him to reassure Anto that he is agreeable to the new arrangement. He returns the ring to her. Git follows Anto into a room where he has been led by two local thugs. While saving his friend from a beating, Git injures the thugs, putting out the eye of one of them, Johnner.

The second section is titled "This is what I need you to do to make it right" (*IWD*, 9). The following morning in the bar, Anto pleads with Tom French for Git, saying he didn't understand the situation. But Tom silences him and says that, to make up for what he did to Johnner, Git will need to pick up some money from a Frank Grogan, who is described as an "associate" "down in Cork doing a deal for me". First he is to take "A friendly face" from Gort "down to Grogan" (11–12). Anto is held hostage as Bunny Kelly arrives to accompany Git. Their first stop is Bunny's house, where he fails to persuade his wife to let him in. After Bunny robs a petrol station, he steals an old car, which quickly stalls.

The next title, which was added to McPherson's screenplay in the completed film, declares "A rendezvous with a friendly face". After Git falls in a pit as they walk through a boggy marsh, they miss their connection at an old garage. They fight over whether they need to find the "friendly face" before they contact Grogan. Frustrated, Bunny declares, "No guts, no black pudding. And I think you know what I'm talking about." Git responds that such quips are "not an argument" (*IWD*, 25). Another added title says they are now in "Cork". At a pub, the Black and Amber, Git shows a picture of Grogan and is escorted to a room where Grogan is supposedly "waiting for you" (28). Bunny is reading a western paperback in the car as Git comes from the pub with blood streaming from his face.

The following section opens with the title "Attentive care and advice. Some reconnaissance. Instruction in firearms. A daring rescue!" (*IWD*, 28). In a hotel room, after Bunny works on Git's nose, Bunny evades talking about his connection to French as they tail the barman to a country house. While they wait, Bunny instructs Git in the use of the revolver and adds that he will charge Git £100 for each bullet used to help "keep a bit of distance" (34). More to the point, Bunny shows Git how to intimidate people with the gun, pushing the younger man in the muck and screaming obscenities at him. To his assertion that the gun is useless "unless you make them believe you're just about fucked up to use it", Git replies, "I think you *are* fucked up" (35).

The next morning, the two men surprise the sleeping criminals and rescue Grogan, who says he doesn't know where the money is. They bundle him into the car boot. From a phone box, they call Tom French's place. Johnner instructs them to take Frank to his friend. Later, they release Frank from the boot, placing him in the back seat, with his hands tied. Frank is genuinely confused about the kidnapping, though he says if Tom French is behind it, it's because "I've been fucking his wife for about eighteen months" (*IWD*, 41). When Git seems potentially sympathetic to Grogan, Bunny stops the car and reminds Git that they have a job to do.

While they work at changing cars yet again, Bunny calls his house, but his wife won't talk to him and his niece won't even "tell Auntie Teresa that Uncle Bunny loves her" (43).

In yet another car, Frank says he does not know the friendly face and warns of French's ruthlessness, in the process calling himself Frank Grogan BA. He continues to plead his case, saying he is "from a lovely family" and believes there's "no gift like giving" (*IWD*, 45–46). While Bunny gets new clothes for Frank, Git tells Frank that he wouldn't let French's man "take care of" Frank (48). Frank replies that he is depending on Git. When they are stopped at a crash scene, the tension builds as the Guard points out that the tax on the car is two months out of date. Frank prolongs the conversation unnecessarily and is rewarded with another visit to the boot.

The next section is titled "Back on the bog. A dirty deal, and then a cleaner deal" (*IWD*, 53). At an old garage next to the bog, Git takes Frank to meet a man who identifies himself as the contact person. But Frank tells Git the man is not "a friendly face" (56) and "I'll be on your conscience forever if you leave me" (57). The contact then draws a gun and disarms Git, but Bunny rescues them. After they deposit the contact man in the boot of his own car, they return to their car, where Frank explains that he has one side of forgery plates for $20 notes. French has the other side. He was to meet French's wife and receive £25,000 in up-front money, but she didn't show. They then call French, who agrees to meet them in the morning.

The following section is called "Some TV. Some R&R. A discourse on aesthetics. A terrible secret. Some dancing and some sexual intercourse" (*IWD*, 64). They check into a hotel and leave Frank tied to the bed watching educational TV, which maddens him. In the bar, Bunny confesses that Tom French is blackmailing him over Bunny's relationship with his cell mate when imprisoned. Bunny adds that he's "not queer, you know" (70). Git responds, "Don't worry about it" (71).

After they meet two women in the bar, Git takes one of them to his room while Bunny surreptitiously tries to listen outside. Bunny then tries to call his wife again, but no one answers. After Git has sex with the girl, he tells her the reason he was imprisoned: he took the fall for his father in a robbery attempt. Bunny also wakes up in bed with a woman, but the interlude is disrupted when Bunny and Git discover that Frank has untied himself and fled.

The next section is titled "The value of an education. A shoot-out and a chase with more shooting" (*IWD*, 80). They find Frank at another hotel, Bunny calling himself "Professor F. Fucking Kelly" who will give "a lecture in gunshot wounds to the face" as he attacks Frank in the bath, naming him a "tubby little no dick lying little fucker" (80–81). As they take Frank to get his clothes, men from Cork arrive outside. After the three escape through the restaurant, Frank is forced once again into the boot as Git fires the gun over the heads of the Cork men. During the ensuing chase, Git shoots the windscreen of the pursuing van, forcing the Cork men to crash across the road. Bunny congratulates Git on his marksmanship but adds that there will be a charge for the bullets and "I don't want to have to be teaching you about ethics on top of everything else" (86).

Finally arriving at their rendezvous, Frank leads them to the woods, where Tom appears, carrying a shovel. At a marked tree, Git digs for a suitcase and in another location finds the box with the counterfeit plate, along with human remains which Tom identifies as those of Sonny Mulligan. In a flashback, Tom and Frank explain that Sonny got the plates from overseas but they had a falling out because Tom and Frank wanted to print more that £50,000. Sonny discovered Frank spying on him and Frank shot Sonny. They then concocted a story that Sonny disappeared with the plates. Back in the present time, Tom pulls a gun and shoots Frank, for Sonny and his wife, he says. Tom calls Bunny "the faggot"

(*IWD*, 97) and shoots him in the shoulder. After fumbling with the gun, Git shoots Tom.

The final section is titled "Sometimes the benefit of the doubt can even save your life" (*IWD*, 98). After burying the bodies in Sonny Mulligan's grave, Git walks away with Bunny leaning on his shoulder. Bunny invites Git to stay at his house for £30 a week, insisting that having money isn't going to change him. There is an "Epilogue" (101) in which Bunny, now well-heeled, approaches Sabrina in the snooker hall. He says he is going to the States. When she asks about Git, he hands her an envelope, saying it contains a "few bob, for you and Head the Ball" (102) from Git, who, he says, has also gone to the US. Bunny assures here that Tom French "did a Sonny Mulligan" (103). She gives him the ring, to which he responds "be ready to forgive your man. Because sometimes the benefit of the doubt can even save your life" (103). Bunny kisses her on the cheek and leaves the snooker hall, crossing to a new BMW driven by Git. Inside the car, Git says he didn't want the ring and calls Bunny a "fucking moron" (104). The film ends with their conversation about oral sex.

This film is not Conor McPherson's most personal work. As with most films, it was a collaborative process from start to finish, and naturally involved compromises on all sides. It was not his idea and the other filmmakers repeatedly asked him to work in directions, both literally and figuratively, that were not of McPherson's choosing. But he was comfortable with collaboration and satisfied with the result. Most importantly, the story, even after all the revisions and bows to American genre movies, left room for the writer to pursue his creative obsessions. Most obviously, there is characteristic McPherson mischief in the title. It is taken from the opening of Plato's *Republic*, which McPherson uses perversely by setting up the film, and the audience, for the sexual joke at the conclusion:

Bunny	D'you remember that bird you were with that night in the hotel?
Git	Yeah . . .
Bunny	Did she suck your cock?
Git	That what's been on your mind?
Bunny	You know . . . I reflect . . . about things. Did she?
Git	Mmhm.
Bunny	Yeah?
Git	But I went down, as well. (Short pause.) I always do. (*IWD*, 104–5)

As risqué as they are, the final lines are more than a male bonding rap. Having comically associated philosophy with cunnilingus and fellatio, the writer interjects a lesson on ethics, specifically the value of mutuality in sexual politics. Typical of McPherson, the obscenity is linked with a call for fair play, sexual and otherwise.

Also typical of McPherson's work is the "profane duet for dissonant voices" played by Bunny and Git, two incomplete, unintegrated men (Morgenstern, 1998: A16). Most obviously, Bunny, as described by his creator, is "a man who *thinks* he's intelligent and he needs to learn that he's not as clever as he thinks he is. In other words, he has a lack of humility. [. . .] For instance, whenever Bunny tries to justify his actions or list reasons for doing something. He'll say the same thing three times in a row without realising it. He pushes forward to the end of a hopelessly repetitive argument" (*IWD*, 116). He is a logical argument waiting to happen. For example, at one point, Bunny interrupts Frank's description of life with French's wife by resorting to one of his many attempts at logic: "we don't know if . . . (Counting on his fingers): One, you're bullshitting us. Two if you're lying, or three, what the fuck is going on" (50). Less obvious, but no less real, is Git's mechanical adherence to reason rather than effective action. Again in McPherson's words, Git "is the more reasonable character, and because he's so reasonable, so loyal, he gets himself in trouble" (Duane, 1997: 15). Given their limitations, the two men are forced to learn the utility of trust:

> We have a man of action, Bunny, and a man of rea-
> sonableness, Git. Bunny has unpremeditated knee-jerk
> responses. Git's responses are more considered. But
> neither of them solely working upon their own in-
> stincts separately can ever achieve anything. Bunny
> nearly lands them both in prison in the first few min-
> utes of their journey because of his impulse to steal.
> But Git almost gets himself killed trying to save
> Grogan. It's only Bunny's protection that saves him.
> So their journey is one of learning to trust each
> other's natural skills. (*IWD*, 116)

Once they learn to co-operate, they become "a useful team, and though their emotional lives are unresolved, at least they have the wherewithal to deal with it" (Duane, 1997: 15).

In a film that required both collaboration and compromise, the two central characters embody the primary issues and emotional conflicts in all McPherson's work. Git is a naturally loyal and reasonable man. But he lacks a playful sense of the rhythms of life. In his adventure with Bunny, Git discovers that mischief, often realised sexually, is life-giving, as long as "going down" from Plato (in the sense of "taking the rap" for his father, or travelling south to Cork, or visiting a Dantesque gangster hell) also leads to fair play, especially with and toward women. Bunny is a creature of impulse and aggression. But in his time with Git, Bunny also begins to sense the value of thinking ethically. Though he could never put the issue into words, he senses a moral imperative, the need to travel up to Plato from the nether regions. Much of the humour in the film is based on his fitful attempts to understand himself and act responsibly toward others on the basis of his own vision of right and wrong. That he doesn't establish a systematic view which he can share with Git and the audience is not the issue. *I Went Down* dramatises the most human attempts of the characters to be free of traditional repressions, to make mischief, while acting responsibly enough with others to have a reasonable chance of experiencing love.

Within the parameters established by his collaborators, McPherson was also able to reassert his belief in the primacy of storytelling. The plot turns on remembered stories, such as the flashback in which Frank and Tom, in voiceover, explain images of their past with Sonny Mulligan, including Tom's marriage to Sonny's niece, their falling-out over counterfeit plates, Frank's murder of Sonny, the lie they fabricate to explain Sonny's disappearance, and the corroboration of Frank's affair with Tom's wife (*IWD*, 94–96). Even more reminiscent of McPherson's plays is Git's explanation to his girlfriend, in the unedited version, of why he went to prison:

> Ah. It was . . . stupid. I . . . took me dad out for a few drinks one night, last year. And he was. All his life, emphysema, couldn't work or that. Loved his drink. But a terrible messy fucking drinker. And I took him out. Lashed a few scoops back, and I was walking home with him. And we saw these cun . . . these fellas ram, ram-raid a shop. A, an electrical shop. Alarms going. The works. They grabbed hi-fis and all this. Into their car and off they went. And this fucking eejit beside me, says he wants a video. Walks into the shop. And picks one up. And I was trying to get him to leave it down, and the guards came and snared us by the cacks. Down the cop shop, the whole bit. They put the video in a bag as evidence and everything. And eh . . . I said I'd done it . [. . .] I was looking at the old fella. He didn't even know what the fuck was going on. Singing rebel songs at the guards and all this. He

was . . . my dad you know. He couldna . . . he was too
weak. So I said it was me. Went up before this bollocks of a judge. And I'd been in a little bit of trouble
years and years before. Messing only, like. Sent me
down for eight months. And then two weeks later I
got word. The old lad kicked it anyway. Heart. Waste
of fucking time. And, I was getting a loan for my . . .
girlfriend. She was gonna go to her . . . sister's wedding. In Australia. And you know, I couldn't . . . get
the loan then. The . . . Credit Union. So . . . And that's
how I lost my girlfriend. (75–76)

Like McPherson's monologues, *I Went Down* uses talk to reveal the characters' compulsions, dependencies, and taste for
the sad and ironic.

But this scene was heavily edited in the released print, indicating an essential difference between storytelling in the
movie versus the plays. In film, the characters no longer need
to attend to the truth of their experience, for themselves or
the audience. As McPherson explains,

[t]he fireworks between Bunny [. . .] and Git [. . .] are
there, but I knew it had to go somewhere, that the
characters had to learn from each other. Being a film
that took its cue from American buddy films and road
movies, it was never going to go as deep as you might
in a play. (Heaney, 1999: 21)

In motion pictures, the job of the narrative is to present the
movie itself, not simply the reflections of its most provocative
characters. In McPherson's words, in the "ambiguous space of
theatre, with '500 people having 500 different impressions of
what's going on'", the audience creates an imagined story
from a fixed storyline. But the "visual tyranny" of film is predi-
cated on a more flexible script that finally gives way to the
collaboration between artists who must deal with the exigen-
cies of shooting and the demands of genre (21).

Saltwater

Conor McPherson has a fascination with contemporary music. Before becoming a playwright and filmmaker, he played in a number of rock bands as a teenager. Even after his own shift from guitar-playing to writing, he continued to follow the careers of artists like Natalie Merchant, Aimee Mann, Ron Sexsmith, Matthew Sweet and Steve Earle (White, 1998: par. 13; "Conor McPherson: Interview", 2001: par. 6). So he was especially attentive when Hand-Made Films, the English production company, showed an interest in filming *This Lime Tree Bower*. McPherson jumped at the chance because, as he admits:

> I thought they were still owned by George Harrison! I hadn't realised the company had changed hands, but by then I had decided to make the film — the prospect of meeting George Harrison nudged me in that direction (McKenzie, 2001a: par. 11).

He sold the rights to Hand-Made in 1996, with Robert Walpole and Treasure Films designated as Irish co-producers. But Hand-Made, according to McPherson, was

> in the middle of trying to develop a sitcom like *Seinfeld* or *Friends* that would run for ever. They spent so much money on it that they went bankrupt. My script was regarded as an asset and passed over to the receiver, a Canadian bank, who wouldn't let us have it. "You're a bank. What good is a screenplay to you?" I asked. "As long as it's of some use to you, it's of some use to us." We had to get a loan and buy it back (Carty, 2000a: 2).

Walpole and McPherson bought back the rights in late 1998 and had the film in production by March of the following year.

As Walpole says in the production notes to *Saltwater*, "With *I Went Down* we wanted to create a very heightened 'silly' film in a way. *Saltwater* is warmer, more human, more embedded in a set of real characters to whom real stuff is happening" (*Saltwater* Press Release, 2000: 11). Such authenticity followed from McPherson's opening "the whole town out more and [. . .] establishing the sense of place [. . .] simply by being able to show it" (6). But the film was not intended to be local colour, a realistic portrait of life in a seaside town outside Dublin. What appealed to McPherson, as he explained in an interview with Will McKenzie, was capturing in a single location the drama of loss. He has had a lifelong interest in such towns as "powerful, evocative places of energy and happiness". Drawn to drama, not static images, he is intrigued by the transition from all that visible and active joy to its absence. In film, he could capture not just a literal place but a "sense of emptiness when that life leaves a place" (McKenzie, 2001a: par. 13).

The film opens with shots establishing this contrast between energy and emptiness in a seaside town, off season, and then in a chip shop with a flat above. In the flat, there is a poker game in progress. At the table are the main characters from *This Lime Tree Bower*: George Beneventi, in his fifties, his three children — Frank (early twenties), Joe (sixteen), and Carmel (late twenties) — and Ray, Carmel's boyfriend. They are drinking beers, except for Joe, who has Pepsi, and George, who has whiskey. When Ray goes for more beer, everyone else cheats, looking for better cards while he is gone. As they resume, George admits he cheated, and Ray follows by wanting to know if they all cheated. As the titles run, the day begins for the family plus Ray.

The story which unreels in this place is generally the same as that in *This Lime Tree Bower*. Joe's feelings toward his mother are visualised in home-movie-like flashbacks that appear as interjected dreams. Ray is still a heavy-drinking womaniser who declares his intention to bring down Wolfgang Konigsberg and regurgitates at the old man's lecture. As in the play, Joe follows Damien, who is harassed by Mr Fanning, the teacher, and plots his petty revenge. At the chipper, Simple Simon and his nephew, Charlie Dunne, are fawned over by George as Frank pleads with his father to not "be wiping your hands for that pig" (S, 31) and subsequently carries out his robbery. Once again Joe and Damien visit the Shadows, and afterwards Damien attacks a girl in a graveyard.

As in *Lime Tree*, Frank once again robs the bookies in a silly costume and escapes from Charlie over the wall, where he runs across Ray and ducks into his car. Despite feelings of guilt, Ray still pursues his student, here identified as Deborah McCeever, against even his own judgement. After the vomiting scene, the three visit a posh hotel, as they did in the plays. And, upon their return, the drama builds over whether the police have arrived about the burglary. Finally, as before, Frank needs to leave, though for an unspecified destination. There will be financial security as long as the family endures some separation, the same dilemma that finishes *This Lime Tree Bower*.

But the film does not end with Joe saying things just got better, as in the play. Indicative of the first major shift in emphasis from theatre to film, *Saltwater*'s concluding scene shows Joe riding his bike near the school, seeing Tara, and walking bike-in-hand up to her, the two young people facing each other, speechless, as the image fades. Visually, McPherson leads the audience to this moment by showing Joe observing her as he repeatedly passes the bus stop. Their potential intimacy is further established when Joe helps Tara look for her bag at the nightclub and tries to support her when she is thrown out by a bouncer and accosted outside by hooligan boys. Consequently, Joe and Damien are given less film time, which deemphasises Joe's infatuation with him as well as the oedipal tensions between Damien and his mother, which bothered Joe in the play. Instead, *Saltwater* foregrounds Damien as an action figure, as when he knocks Mr Fanning and Mr Gibney, the teachers, to the ground with a stone.

Added to the narrative is Sergeant Duggan, a female detective, played by Gina Moxley. A sensitive and bright policewoman, Duggan intuits both the innocence of Joe and the guilt of Frank. Her role is complicated by her attraction for Frank. She not only asks him to join the guards as a way of increasing his self-esteem; she invites him to visit a new night place out in Lusk. When he hesitates, she replies, "Don't have a heart attack. And forget I asked" (S, 25). But Frank is defensive, distrusting her encouragements and believing Duggan, as a representative of public authority, secretly wants to humiliate the Beneventi family. While the Sergeant engages Frank teasingly and is able to clear Joe of the charges, she is never able to gain the confidence of Frank, either in love or in the pursuit of social justice.

The addition of Sergeant Duggan indicates McPherson's desire to develop the texture of life in the seaside town. In the chipper, Larry, a town drunk, accosts Duggan for arresting what he calls "republicans [. . .] trying to set poor old Ireland free" (S, 23). At Reynolds Bar, Frank has a pint and listens to Mack and Larry, two other drinkers, reminisce about a once beautiful girl who is now fat and ugly. "To see her now? . . . You'd nearly shit yourself", Larry declares. To which Mack adds, "It'd break your heart" (48). Similarly, McPherson develops complexity at the college, where Ray's colleague and adversary, Trish Meehan, endures his insults in order to offer him a friendly warning about his involvement with the student: "Sort it out, Ray. Don't make me tell Tony [Regan, the department head]" (94).

Family life also gains humour and warmth in the translation from stage to screen. The sister Carmel, as played by Valerie Spelman, invites Ray to confess his philandering, but when he refuses, she seems self-confident and independent. The same assuredness inspires her to ask, upon discovering

Frank practising for the hold-up, if he is "having a bit of a play" (*S*, 61–62). Brian Cox, as the father George, is revealed as alternately anxious and playful in his interaction with the boys. For example, late in the film, George picks up a photo of his wife and explains to Joe that the mother was partially deaf in one ear, apparently from a baby tooth she put under her pillow as a child. George tries to take it from his wallet but finds he has lost the tooth. A small but resonant moment, the scene pictures the men opening up to each other about their past, sharing a joke, and revelling in the absurdity and losses in their lives.

As that scene suggests, the writer/director is also willing to suspend the forward movement of the plot in order to explore with his actors what François Truffaut once called "privileged moments". The most indulgent and comical scene in *Saltwater* is the hold-up. Peter McDonald, as Frank, not only dons the bobble hat with the cut out eyes; the anxiety of his new aggression strangles his voice. Trying to be threatening, he can only stumble out "Nodiddy fuckdinove" (*S*, 73). A couple of moments later one old man, hearing that his horse has won a race, incongruously exclaims "Yes" (75). Frank then tells Simple Simon (Brendan Gleeson) to take his clothes off, which he partially does, and finally pushes Simon onto the street. During their temporary flight from the seaside town, the three men visit a nightclub, where Ray catches Joe watching a particular girl dance and fetches her back to the table, introducing her as Michelle. As the two youngsters get up to dance, Frank asks how Ray enticed Michelle. He says he told her Joe had six months to live. When Frank asks if she won't be worried about catching it, Ray says, "You can't catch leukaemia" (109).

Thematically, *Saltwater* reprises the dialectic between the physical and the spiritual that informed *This Lime Tree Bower*. Ray, the most perverse of the characters, nevertheless helps Joe find intimacy and counsels the boy about fair play and personal weakness. At the expensive hotel, in the sauna Joe asks Ray about what a girl wants when she's with a man. Ray responds that it is like asking what people want and the only rule is to not be a bollocks — "but you probably will anyway". Then he adds, "I wish I'd respected women more in my life. Because nothing's worth ending up on your own for. Nothing" (S, 105). Caught between compulsion and conscience, he admits to Carmel that he doesn't think about her enough and yet his difficulty with change is implied in his response to Frank in the last scene: "You know me" (62–63, 120–21). At the same time, there is a transcendent world of emotional connection which is available to these men through sharing memories of their mother and her love. As McPherson says, the discovery of the mother's tooth acts as "a tiny connection to the spirit world for Joe and George, a suggestion of their mortality which binds them to Maria finally even though they've been anxious to avoid talking about her before" (139). But they mostly deny or run from those realities.

The script and McPherson's comments on the film make explicit a number of other issues in *Saltwater*. For example, in a lecture by Ray that was edited from the film, the primal tension between desire and ethics is made explicit. Hedonist that he is, Ray nevertheless explains to his class, "What reason governs is our will. Reason stops us merely doing what we want, when we want. It's the moment of reflection. The moment of pause in the moment of passion. The moment we could say, of humanity" (S, 44). By putting these truthful words in the mouth of Ray, the screenwriter added a layer of emotional and dramatic significance to the film (at least before editing). As he explained to Will McKenzie, McPherson was expressing in *Saltwater*

> the difference between what these "thinkers" ought to be doing: considering issues of human emotions; what it actually means to be human; approaching is-

sues of ethics and politics and what they were doing
— getting involved in issues of personal ambition.
(2001a: par. 19)

In the same discussion, he clarifies his position on Professor
Konigsberg's lecture in the film:

I'm very wary about people who proclaim that
"everything is gone", or "everything is finished". How
can he say that language is dead when he's using language when communicating that very idea? (par. 21).

Strikingly similar to the trip of the young people to the
sea described in *Port Authority*, *Saltwater*, more than *This Lime
Tree Bower*, is a study of the turning back that follows the inevitable boundaries in human experience. As much as many of
McPherson's characters are energised by moving beyond traditional rules, they eventually are faced with ethical dilemmas,
either of conscience or action. Ray is able to name his issue: if
he continues his betrayal of his relationship with Carmel, he
will end up alone, his most frightening prospect. Frank learns
how to avoid the family curse of impotence, which George
calls being observers rather than initiators, but in the end he
must accept the consequences of his illegal acts. Joe, despite
his sweet temper, is required to accept the real politic of the
human community — that most people will betray others to
preserve or assert their own interests. When George and Joe
glance at the salt water in the final scenes, they begin to
sense, along with sensitive viewers, that some borders are
finally non-negotiable. They have come to the place where
ethics and morality begin. *Saltwater* is filmed on the boundary
where mischief is being transformed into the responsible
world where it is necessary, even desirable, to be the "good
man" George applauds Joe for becoming when the boy takes
a blood test to prove his innocence (*S*, 116).

Conor McPherson's adaptation of his play *This Lime Tree Bower* into the film *Saltwater* suggests the essential difference in the way he approaches theatrical and film drama. In film, he says,

> the script isn't paramount. The crux of the difference between theatre and film is that when you're writing a film script you imagine it as perfect, but then when you're shooting you don't have time; suddenly you have to reconceive and you're basically putting square pegs into round holes. (Heaney, 1999: 21)

If the director is lucky, as he insists he was on *Saltwater*, he includes "great performances and great ideas from the actors" in the filming process. And finally, "when you're editing a film you find it has its own internal rhythm. It ends up a co-operative venture" (21). As he discovered during his involvement with *I Went Down*, such collaboration inevitably leaves the script, even one conceived as "perfect", on the set.

Plays, he believes, are essentially conservative in their call to reason and empathy. Whether articulated by a single actor/character or an ensemble, their stories rely on an imagined past which encourages the audience to share the life of the actor — literally his character. In such an environment, the speakers can travel anywhere and say whatever they want, as long as they are engaging. Film, according to McPherson, has little of this faith. Celluloid people freely assert their identity, but they do not share it. The truth of the past is lost on movies which offer instead the purifying fire of the present, which requires the characters to curb their impulses to indulge in freewheeling talk. The story can be trusted in both cases, but the essential alienation of movie-going frees the audience from the past. The compassion of theatre gives way to film's judgement and eroticism.

As McPherson suggests in his "Notes on Postproduction", such a shift requires the director to be especially cognisant of the role of the audience in the politics of filmmaking. In plays he expects, and needs, responses based on aesthetic distance, sensitive observance, and reasonable judgement. In film, the viewers are even less likely to use their reason, to practise thoughtful response, because of the tightly constructed plots, which are designed to stimulate vicarious thrills and purely emotional reactions. McPherson feels he and the editor, Emer Reynolds, were successful in controlling such tendencies by working outside the studio system: "Where executives for a studio may try to shore up what they see as holes in the plot, we were able to actively try to create holes and make some space and hopefully allow the audience to make up their own minds as to aspects of the story" (S, 139). The "holes" and "space" represent the writer/director's pursuit of a democratic cinema in which ambiguous words, images, and actions encourage the viewers to make up their own minds about the story. Such opportunities, the writer believes, are much more possible and frequent in independent films.

Recent Film Work

Since *Saltwater,* Conor McPherson has continued his work in film, alongside that in theatre. It was natural that he would direct one of Samuel Beckett's plays, *Endgame,* for Channel Four's "Beckett on Film" series, produced by Blue Angel Films/Tyrone Productions. The director shares with Beckett the humour that comes from revealing the distance between self-importance and the absurdity of individual lives: "What we perceive is very limited, and to watch us walking around like peacocks expounding our theories is comic. That's why I think Beckett was brilliant, showing people right at the edge looking into absolute meaninglessness. How do you face the fact that you might not know anything and you're completely lost?" (Gussow, 1999: B3). As McPherson clarified in the interview in this book, he feels Beckett's work is darker than

McPherson's own, which asserts that the essential "meaning-lessness" and confusion of things can be the basis of authentic and empathetic relationships. Nevertheless, he was willing to follow Beckett's instructions in filming a careful, moving, and often humorous rendition of the Beckett play, starring Michael Gambon and David Thewlis, with Charles Simon and Jean Anderson. The director of photography was Donal Gilligan, with costuming by Consolata Boyle and set design by Clodagh Conroy. The editor was Mary Finlay.

The result is a film, though made within the restrictions of Beckett's estate and expressing Beckett's own dark view, which has more McPherson touches than just the emphasis on humour. Beckett's interior space is imagined as a bare attic, reminiscent of the nearly empty stages of McPherson's monologues. As in *Port Authority*, bells sound in the air, reinforced by coldly mechanical noises and exhaling from an unknown source. Under McPherson's direction, *Endgame* toys with the metaphor and conventions of playmaking. Hamm's declaration "Me — to play" echoes throughout the film, as do the markers "Something is taking its course" and "We're getting on", suggesting a drama which self-consciously lives outside traditional structures. From the perspective of both McPherson's monologues and Beckett's *Endgame*, only parody and the mock-heroic are honest responses to literary pretensions to "chronicle", "technique", "complications", and "underplot". In the cases of both writers, attempts to gain order and purpose by storytelling (here, Nagg and the trousers, Hamm and the hungry child) are troubled by the loss of cultural and linguistic contexts for their words. These characters, like those of the director of the film, live on the margins between the modern call to identity and the post-modern celebration of rudderless licence.

More indicative of McPherson's tastes as a filmmaker is the focus, as in *Saltwater*, on the human face. From the initial slow zoom out to Clov's face in profile, the film studies the character's reactions, their connection in depth, employing staccato cuts to showcase the human form against stark and lifeless backgrounds. Moments of prolonged expression are typically caressed by long, slow pans, usually from left to right, which invite the viewer to gaze at the actor/character in isolation and reflection. These are the faces of belligerent but lonely men, like McPherson's, needing family connections for solace but mechanically denying such loving affection. Caught between assertion and repression, they fear that love's utility will finally exclude them. As Hamm tells Clov, their pitiless existence will come home to roost: "Yes, one day [. . .] you won't have anyone with you, because you won't have had pity on anyone and because there won't be anyone left to have pity on." That is Ray's primary anxiety in *Saltwater*.

At the heart of Conor McPherson's attraction to *Endgame* are the limits of intelligence and the inevitability of masks. Having been convinced by his study of philosophy that no one really knows anything for sure, the director highlights Hamm's humorous command that Clov have "An idea [. . .] A bright idea", despite the pains in his legs. Clov's proud response is that the absence of an alarm will indicate his death to Hamm. Without mental grounding or clear motives, the Beckett characters are condemned to masks, indicated by the rag Hamm wears over his head at the beginning and end of the play, which may have inspired the bags in *Come On Over*. As in a McPherson play, the characters are half-aware of their sad interior condition as they imagine a freer, more peaceful exterior. While McPherson's own plays exhibit more respect for language and morality, both writers are drawn to the tragicomic use of stories, ideas and the human face, haunted by loss, isolation and silence.

After *Endgame*, McPherson committed to a project with Neil Jordan, *The Actors*. The idea belonged to Jordan, who tried to write the story as a novel. But with all the complications in the storyline, Jordan felt *The Actors* might work better as a film, which McPherson agreed to write. Once the people at the studio saw *Saltwater*, they agreed that he should direct as well. The writer/director describes the film as "a sort of old-fashioned Ealing comedy about actors. They get themselves into trouble. This actor who's not very good ends up having to play six different parts and juggle the whole situation they're in to get them out of trouble." He adds that the major obstacle was DreamWorks wanting an American actor, though Jordan was very supportive of McPherson's position, which was to keep the film from being "set in Philadelphia" (Carty, 2000a: 2). DreamWorks dropped the film, but Miramax stepped in, and it was shot in Dublin in early 2002 and released in May 2003.

The basic storyline concerns two actors, named O'Malley (played by Michael Caine) and Tom (played by Irish comedian Dylan Moran). O'Malley, an ageing mentor to Tom, has been doing research for the role of Shakespeare's Richard III by visiting gangsters at a pub, particularly a foolish criminal named Barreller (Michael Gambon). Learning that Barreller owes a London gangster, Magnani (Miranda Richardson), O'Malley proposes that they disguise themselves as Magnani's men and intercept the money, which Tom reluctantly agrees to after his home burns. When the heist is botched, Tom, with the help of his niece Mary (Abigail Iversen), is forced to assume a series of characters, a process which develops his acting skills. Further complications follow when Tom becomes attracted to Barreller's daughter, Dolores (Lena Headey), and Magnani travels from London to recover her money (*The Actors* Press Release).

The film is set in McPherson's most familiar location, North Dublin, where once again he studies the mischievous and collaborative nature of theatre. Even though the original story was Jordan's, *The Actors* gave the screenwriter/director the opportunity to explore the comic pretensions of vanity and the black humour in identity issues. Like other McPherson work, it takes place at the intersection of explosive rebelliousness and inescapable reality. *The Actors* was produced by Company of Wolves (the Neil Jordan/Stephen Woolley company), with Redmond Morris co-producing. Seamus McGarvey served as director of photography, with production design by Mark Geraghty. The costume designer was Consolata Boyle; make-up was by Veronica Brebner. As on *Saltwater*, editing was by Emer Reynolds. The film is distributed by Filmfour and Miramax Films.

There is also the continuing saga of *MacIntyre*, another film with Breathnach. For that film, McPherson and the director travelled to the American South, particularly Alabama and Georgia, to research a story about a black woman working in a deputy sheriff's office in a small southern town about to celebrate a bicentennial. While studying for the sergeant's exam, she stops a speeder, who it turns out is in a witness protection programme. He also has committed a murder and is being pursued by both the FBI and people who want to assassinate him. The film has been delayed while the director makes *The Actors* and directs the first production of his play *Dublin Carol* in New York. But, as McPherson notes in the interview in this book, *MacIntyre* is still being considered for production. The writer has completed both the research and a draft of the film, which the filmmakers consider even more of a genre film than *I Went Down*.

As this book goes to press, McPherson has indicated that he is working on another script with Neil Jordan, a "buddy road movie" inspired by the journey of the Magi: "The Three Kings: it's like a big epic adventure that hasn't been made" (Clarke, 2003: W7).

Conor McPherson is one of many contemporary artists who work simultaneously in theatre and film. Like Gerry Stembridge and Neil Jordan in Ireland, Mike Leigh in England, and David Mamet, Neil LaBute and Kenneth Lonergan in the United States, he writes for the stage and also directs motion pictures. But McPherson so far has not aspired to be a film stylist or *auteur*, like Jordan and Leigh. He relies heavily on his cinematographers for the visual sense when he directs, and he willingly collaborates with directors and producers when he writes for the screen. Of the group mentioned above, he is closest to Mamet in staying true to the screenplay and the written word. Even then, McPherson is distinguished from that American writer by his non-doctrinaire approach to acting and his interest in opening up his own work to location shooting. More than any other of these playwrights, he is willing to reimagine his work and compose as he shoots, as long as he has the freedoms offered by independent filmmaking.

Chapter Five

Recent Plays: Nowhere Except Towards Each Other

Into the first decade of the new millennium, Conor McPherson continues to work both in theatre and film. Even as he has become involved with writing and directing Irish films for world distribution, he has written a number of plays, all of which show his continuing experimentation with theatrical form and his fascination with the need for a moral response to the new freedoms in the Republic of Ireland. Three of these plays have been produced. In the first, *Dublin Carol*, he followed the more traditional lines of the ensemble theatre. As in *The Weir*, the playwright imagined a single location — a business office — and a series of stories told by three characters, all moving toward self-understanding and inevitable choices. While the setting is as simple as that in *The Weir*, in *Dublin Carol* McPherson creates a more poetic, more resonant situation which borrows from Christian images and rituals. In *Port Authority*, he returned to the monologue, using once again three narrators. But this time they do not share a single story, as in *This Lime Tree Bower*. Instead, McPherson studies how three generations of Irish men confront freedom and loneliness in stories which slightly intersect without building dramatically from each other. Finally, in the one-act *Come On Over*, he leaves the naturalistic theatre behind, imagining a surreal situation in which a priest and his former girlfriend play with various masks of identity and concealment at the intersection of spirituality and physicality.

Dublin Carol

Dublin Carol was first produced at the Royal Court Theatre, in London on 22 February 2000. It was directed by Ian Rickson. Rae Smith was both the set and costume designer. Paule Constable was the lighting designer; sound design was by Paul Arditti, with original music by Stephen Warbeck. Brian Cox played John, Andrew Scott was Mark, and Bronagh Gallagher played Mary. The play was first staged in Ireland at the Gate Theatre in Dublin on 3 October 2000. That production was directed by Liz Ascroft, with lighting designed by Mick Hughes. The cast included John Kavanagh (John), Sean McDonagh (Mark), and Donna Dent (Mary). It premiered in the United States on 4 February 2003 at the Atlantic Theater Company, directed by McPherson and starring Jim Norton, Keith Nobbs and Kerry O'Malley. Sets were by Walt Spangler and Tyler Micoleau was responsible for lighting. The costume designer was Kaye Voyce, with sound by Scott Myers.

The play is in three parts. It is set on Christmas Eve in an "office on the Northside of Dublin, around Fairview or the North Strand Road" (*DC*, 5), which is decorated with "scrawny" (9) Christmas decorations, including a small plastic Christmas tree and an Advent calendar. Mark, a young man, aged about twenty, arrives wearing a black suit and overcoat. He waits dutifully until John, in his fifties, follows. They are both wet. As they make the room comfortable, John takes some whiskey and tells Mark he will have to wait for the tea, which John is fixing. When John asks if Mark has been to The Strand, a local pub, the young man answers yes, with his girlfriend, an airline hostess from Marino named Kim. In a mysterious declaration, John tells Mark he did well in a difficult situation involving a young person who may have been into drugs, with the wife looking angrily at many of the women standing around.

As church bells ring, they admit that neither goes to mass, though John says it feels like he does since there is always mass at the funerals. (It is becoming clear that these men are undertakers.) Mark admits he likes Christmas, and John asks him to open a door on the Advent calendar, little angels in a choir. John says he visited Noel in the hospital the night before and adds that Mark should visit his uncle (Noel) because it would help the job situation. The older man then confesses that he used to have a problem with drink until Noel met him in a bar and sorted him out. As the first part comes to a close, John says the worst death he ever saw was the time a fourteen-year-old girl had given birth and pushed the baby down a toilet. He also remembers a wealthy man who committed suicide peacefully with a statue to Buddha in the room. Telling Mark to come back later for his money, John cleans up and follows Mark out the door, muttering "Buddha" as he leaves (*DC*, 32).

Part two opens with Mary (John's daughter) coming into the office, followed by John. He makes her a whiskey while he drinks two himself. They agree that she will pick him up at five on the way to the hospital, after he has given Mark his wages. He asks about Paul, her brother, and Mary says he is getting along, fixing motorbikes in London with an English chap, though he is acting more like John as he gets older and has a horrible girlfriend. When John asks about her, she says she is working at Dunnes Stores in Stephen's Green and sometimes escapes pointlessly into the country. Her reference to the country stimulates their memory of a family trip to Limerick and the night John did not come home. John declares that the enormity of his mistakes makes the word "sorry" insignificant.

Mary replies that she loves him, that she can't help herself, that she always thinks of him. He lamely says that he thinks about her too. She responds that, compared to him even her worst boyfriend was a mere amateur messer.

The discussion switches to Carol (his girlfriend while he was still married), who John says was too accepting and would have let him kill himself. Then Mary remembers the day he was drunk and took her into a bar, where she hid down under the stool, hoping Jesus would take her away. He says he is sorry and remembers that he almost returned home but instead went on another bender. When he says he sometimes wishes he had never existed, Mary tries to comfort him by saying then she wouldn't exist and, besides, she is somewhat of an eejit on her own. When she asks about his feelings toward her mother, John responds that he often felt sorry for her. Mary assures him that her mother got strength through all this trouble, there was some humour, and that John and her mother would have been good friends if they were the same sex. John philosophises that the only thing that helps is being good like Noel but then he resents the goodness.

When Mary asks what happened to him, he responds with a long list: "Boredom. Loneliness. A feeling of basically being out of step with everybody else. Fear. Anxiety. Tension. And of course, a disposition to generally liking the whole fucking thing of drinking until you pass out" (DC, 59). He analyses that he always felt guilty since he failed to stop his father from beating his mother for fear of being hit himself. Later, he "thought the world was a bad place and that someone was going to come and attack us" (60) and he would not be able to defend them. Mary asks him to do the funeral, but he says he can't. She asks him to at least stop drinking, and he agrees. She promises to return at five o'clock.

Part three opens at four o'clock with John slumping in a chair in a drunken stupor. When Mark enters, John mistakes him for Paul, his son, and admits forgetting the pay for Mark.

John fumbles for his own money, which Mark declines. They start drinking, rationalising that it is Christmas Eve. Mark explains that he tried to break it off with Kim but backed off when she grabbed him and made a pitiful noise. John tries to convince Mark that he was doing the right thing, that Kim was at fault or at least faking her emotions. He adds that he was more attached to the booze than Carol: "I thought of it like God had sent me like a drink-angel." In his mind, unconditional love will hook and pickle you "into torturing yourself" (*DC*, 77). Mark objects by saying John is "doing a bunk" on his family (78) and starts to leave, but John explains that his wife has cancer and he needs a confidant.

John finally commits to visiting his wife in the hospital and confesses that when his son last came from England, John hid to avoid him. Mark starts making tea for John and, at John's suggestion, opens the last door of the advent calendar, which shows Jesus. As they take down the Christmas decorations together, John describes the alcoholic cycle of paranoid hangovers that can only be relieved by more drink and asserts that Noel is better for him than Carol, who fed this cycle of highs and lows. They share a laugh over Mark's worrying and agree to see Noel the next day. As John takes the advent calendar off the wall, they conclude that there should be something like that for the whole year. Then, as he takes out a Walkman, John observes that it would be great if you could clear the static out of people, like when you earth a Walkman. As Mark leaves, he says he is "sorry . . . for your wife" (*DC*, 88). After Mark leaves, John straightens things up, replaces the advent calendar, and starts redecorating as church bells chime for five o'clock.

At the most literal level the title of the play refers to Carol from Dublin, the woman with whom John becomes involved while he is married. She is remarkable for her ability to love without qualification and, more importantly, without judgement. While this reference seems the most superficial,

Carol's selflessness is a major motif in McPherson's recent work, including *Port Authority*. The men seem trapped in a cycle of guilt, especially religiously induced, and look to women who will accept them unconditionally. But in *Dublin Carol*, the playwright also explains that people with addictive problems and mountains of self-loathing also need friends and lovers who will help with boundaries on their behaviour. John could not ultimately respect Carol, and needed to leave her, in search of the more responsible friendship of Noel who adds rules and consistency to a loving nature. John needs more than acceptance; he needs help.

The play also is a Christmas play for contemporary Ireland. As Robert King notes, in the "poetic" title of the play, "'Dublin' can easily replace the normal 'Christmas' because a new secularism, riding economic revival and religious scandal, is replacing the old Irish faith" (King, 2000a: 71). But McPherson is neither a satirist nor a devotee of Charles Dickens. This song at the Christmas season does not focus on transformation, at least not in the radical way of the Dickens novel. John and Mark, inspired by Noel, do find a degree of rapport and openness that is redemptive in a limited way. And John does start to put the Christmas decorations back in order; the spirit of love is saved from obscurity. But closure is not the goal or reality at the end of *Dublin Carol*. John is an alcoholic with serious impulses for flight or self-destruction. He has betrayed other commitments. And Mary, both the literal and figurative one, hasn't arrived at the door yet. He has neither rejoined her nor arrived at the hospital and thus has not demonstrated the courage to face his son.

What has changed is Conor McPherson's approach to mischief. In the sense of dramatic construction, he is less experimental, less interested in betraying traditional theatrical form, less even than he was in *The Weir*. As he explains in the interview at the end of this book, he is also conscious of cutting off John's rationalistic impulses to create a monologue.

Moreover, there is much more psychology, for want of a more exact word, in this play. All the characters, but especially John, explain their personal histories, which are revealed as indicators, in Wordsworth's phrase of "spots of time", which were crucial in shaping their behaviour, including their mischievous impulses. The implication is that these qualities were not healthy, in the rhetoric of this and other recent McPherson plays, not redemptive. Not only should the characters quit the mischief; they need help in doing so. Noel and Mary, who are effective in establishing limits, are better aids to John than Dublin Carol.

The themes of the play are, as Robert King again has identified, "the common [. . .] ones of modern Irish literature: alcohol, religion, death, family, guilt and loss". Within this general orientation, *Dublin Carol* focuses on John's specific contradictions: "He can bury the dead but cannot face his wife's dying; he dominates the others with his long speeches but dodges personal responsibility — failure just 'grabs' him 'by the throat'" (King, 2000a: 71). His failure is not just material. As McPherson himself has identified, it is emotional. He is, he says, "usually writing about the same things all the time, people who are looking to connect with other people" while "feeling guilty that their own selfishness is getting in the way". Such a connection would be, for them, "some kind of salvation". John, like Mark, is just one step from the loving attachment that would bring him peace and order, but he does not believe he deserves such happiness and therefore does not let it happen. In the author's words, "*Dublin Carol* is really just about the difficulty of someone accepting the community around them, and allowing themselves to be part of it, and allowing themselves just to be happy" (Kilroy, 2000: 5).

Once again it is crucial that the audience has a balanced response to such a dilemma. Benedict Nightingale, for example, is properly irritated with John's confession:

> Isn't this repentant sinner wallowing in his remorse?
> Isn't there a point at which self-hatred becomes self-
> indulgence? And how strong a psychological alibi is
> the revelation that John himself had a vicious father?
> For all the talk, you're left sharing the confusions of a
> man who can meticulously describe but not fully un-
> derstand himself. (2000c: AR16)

Given such ambivalence and confusion, a resolution to John's
situation is impossible during the single day imagined in the
play. Paralysed by an unresolved conflict between his mind and
heart, John cannot, as McPherson says of him, "understand
that what's happening to him is beyond his control". At the
same time, he does not have the inner resources to change
himself and embrace loving others around him. What the play
requires, and what some critics do not elicit, is an identification with "the need to project a coping persona when you
might feel you're going to explode", even if that sense of self is
made inauthentic by evasion and remorse (Gussow, 1999: B3).
Audiences who keep their aesthetic distance without con-
demning this somewhat lost man can learn from him, if they
will, from their relatively safe and comfortable seats.

  Dublin Carol is an interesting combination of the McPherson impulses toward the freedom of the monologue and the
morality of the ensemble play. John is an older version of the
earlier monologuists, driven by self-absorption, alcohol, and
garrulousness to seize the stage time for himself and justify
himself to his audience. But, unlike the previous characters,
he cannot escape his long history and uses introspection and
self-analysis more than the single speakers. At the same time,
his social situation is closer to that in *The Weir* than *Rum and
Vodka*, and so he is caught in his act by a daughter who refuses to be alienated from him and a co-worker who notes
his lies and asks for accountability and silence.

The audience for such a play cannot be as indulgent as that for the early monologues or as empathetic as that in *The Weir*. In order to read the play on its own terms, the viewer or reader needs to be less vicarious, more sad and worried for John than it had been for the unnamed speakers. But his insights and his genuinely confessional spirit — towards the other characters, not just the observers beyond the fourth wall — are necessary for any of the redemption he seeks. Finally, the images of Catholicism, especially the unqualified compassion and endless love imagined in the Virgin Mary and Jesus, still abide, though ambiguously, at the end of the play. In the final scene, John stands at the threshold separating his destructive past from the opportunity to live a moral, a good life. Until he takes the action which reveals his intransigence or his courage, final judgement needs to wait with him.

Port Authority

The first production of *Port Authority* was at the New Ambassadors Theatre, London, on 22 February 2001, by the Gate Theatre of Dublin in association with the Ambassador Theatre Group and Old Vic Productions. The play was directed by Conor McPherson, with set and costume design by Eileen Diss and lighting design by Mick Hughes. The actors were Éanna MacLiam as Kevin, Stephen Brennan playing Dermot, and Jim Norton as Joe. *Port Authority* opened in Ireland at the Gate Theatre on 24 April 2001, with McPherson again directing.

The players move on stage with varying degrees of awareness of the audience and sit at odd angles on a small riser toward the back of the stage. They come forward, as in *This Lime Tree Bower*, to speak in turn to the audience. But unlike the characters in the previous play, they tell their own tales exclusively, not sharing a common narrative or, with very small exceptions, history. Impressionistic lighting is offered on a screen at the back. Bells sound as each actor/

character finishes his portion of the play's story. Kevin is the first, a young man of about twenty. He is followed by Dermot, in his thirties, and then Joe, in his seventies.

Kevin begins by explaining that he moved out of his parents' home to share a place in Donnycarney with three other young people. He admits, "Moving out was like pretending to make a decision" (*PA*, 11). His roommates include Davy Rose, who is usually drunk, and Speedy, mostly Davy's friend, who Kevin feels "definitely had a learning disorder or something" and was "excited by being bored" (11). Since Davy had been dumped "by this girl with blue hair from Beaumont" (12), Kevin takes him to an off-licence. Kevin asks about Clare, the fourth roommate, who is loved by everyone in Dublin and tends to go out with "headbangers. Or lads who thought they were, anyway" (12). In the morning, while watching breakfast TV, Speedy tells how the previous Friday he was having a "sneaky ride" with a "goth girl" while her boyfriend played with a band in the next room (13). She started making too much noise, so Speedy left to masturbate in the toilet. Bored, Kevin confides to the audience:

> I was just sitting there staring at the side of his head, thinking that there was nothing he could ever say that could interest me beyond the terrible notion that I cared absolutely nothing for this fellow human being. And that if he died I'd feel nothing. (13)

Speedy does, however, say that Clare has arrived.

Dermot begins by describing a dinner party welcoming him into his new company. In his last job, he says, the men were embarrassed by their wives' hysteria and watching of *Eastenders*. For this new position, he purchased expensive clothes and told his wife the party was not for wives, even though the executives' wives would be there. He believes Mary (his wife) was meant more for taking care of their nine-year-old son Colm, who is sickly and bullied at school.

O'Hagan, the new boss, had personally called Dermot about the job; this time, he says, "it was going to happen" (*PA*, 15).

Joe begins his monologue by explaining that he awoke that morning with an unusual appetite. "Sister Pat" was carrying a little box wrapped in brown paper, which had been delivered to his son's house and then brought over by Lisa, the son's wife. It is not his birthday, he explains. And Sister Pat, like a little girl, wanted him to open it, but he said he would wait until after breakfast. As Lisa leaves, the nun calls him vain, but he admits to the audience that she was actually very good for "a religious" (*PA*, 16). When he says he put on his jacket and got his stick ready, it is clear that he is in a home for the elderly. In the twenty-person home, he sits down for breakfast with the usual people, Jackie Fennel and Mary Larkin. While Mary talks about her son and his wife, Jackie reads the racing section in the *Independent*. After everyone else leaves, over tea he unwraps the package, which has a handwritten note and a small photo which he recognises. "And I knew what had happened", he concludes, "and I didn't need to read the note" (18).

Kevin picks up his story with a visit to Clare, who is considering redecorating her room. She is, he says, "subtly sexy and easy to be with". She asks him to listen to a demo CD of her boyfriend's (Declan's) band, and Kevin is disappointed when they are actually good. So he suggests that Davy's band, The Bangers, play with them sometime. That night they are at a bus stop on the Malahide Road: "It was a gorgeous summer's evening. All amber and a cool breeze. Clare had one of her runners off shaking a little stone out of it" (*PA*, 21). She asked him if he was all right. He said he was fine.

Returning to his story, Dermot says that his wife, Mary, dropped him off at the train to Sutton Cross for the party. He waited until she had left and then went down to the bar for a few gin and tonics. When he arrived at his stop, he also headed to the Marine Hotel for a few more drinks before finally arriving at the home of O'Hagan, a financial manager for important artists and a celebrity himself. He is ushered in by a blonde girl with a strapless dress, who offers him champagne as she leads him into the drawing room. He has two more drinks before O'Hagan's wife comes to take him to dinner. He feels awkward, as O'Hagan's wife's breasts are visible in her pink dress, but he is so drunk he fixates on them like an astronaut looking to "a vital NASA supply" for "balance" (*PA*, 25). He is not responding to questions, just wants to go to the toilet, and thinks people have X-ray eyes that can see into him.

Next, Joe describes life in his day as unselfconscious and normal: "I never thought about myself. I saw the world as a very organised place that was easy to negotiate. I saw people as generally good and if there were blackguards around the place — well that's what they were. Blackguards" (*PA*, 27). He met his wife, Liz, while he was still living with his parents and working at Cadbury's. He asked her to the Christmas dance in 1956; she was "Always laughing. Always in good form" and he "could easily stand in her parents' living room at Christmas time and she could easily sit in mine" (27). So they got married in 1960, moved to Donnycarney, where they established a quiet life. Their son, Stephen, was born in 1961 and their daughter, Tania, two years later. As things improved they moved to a nicer place in Sutton. Then he declares, "I've no idea about myself! I don't even know if I'm happy or sad!" (28).

Kevin then moves the audience forward to a night in which The Bangers are the headliners, but one band, The Lepers, doesn't show because a player had lost a finger in a sheet metal accident. There were a lot of jokes about the leper losing his finger, Kevin adds. The Bangers argue over whether to go on, which is especially embarrassing for Clare because her boyfriend, Declan, is there, "Into that whole suede jacket, jeans and boots vibe. Big sideburns on him" (*PA*, 29). Davy's solution to the unhappiness is to arrange a housewarming party in two weeks. When The Bangers decide to go on, Kevin retreats to a bar where the barmaid awakens him from a stupor by slapping him across the face. Later, the girl, named Trish, joins them at a diner.

Dermot picks up his story with a bit of advice: don't try to work things out because things and people aren't normal. He is sitting in the toilet at the party, thinking he had blown everything, when O'Hagan's wife asks him if he's OK, with no punishment or judgement in her voice. So he opens the door. And the others welcome him back to the table, which makes him think that things are different among the wealthy and royalty. They hired him, he remembers, when he didn't pass his ACCA, made no sales at a car dealer, and was sacked for homosexual harassment. They offer him cigars and invite him to a concert by The Bangers, which O'Hagan calls the next big Irish band, in Los Angeles on St Patrick's Day weekend. Dermot says that he can either take that trip or go to Mary's mother's house for corned beef and cabbage and hard potatoes.

Joe resumes his story with advice as well. He says to never dream of love because if you do, you'll find the person and that will disturb the world for an ordinary man. He then returns the audience to Sutton and a party at the home of their neighbours, Tommy and Marion Ross. At ten o'clock, Joe is getting a sandwich and talking to Marion in the kitchen — perfectly innocent, except the night before he had dreamed of being down by a river with a dark-haired woman who offered him "unconditional no-nonsense acceptance" (*PA*, 36). Even though Marion has fair hair and a pug nose, he becomes enamoured of the way her face moves and her leg twists. The rest of the night he tries to attribute the twitches in his arms and legs to the Smithwicks and assure himself that God hasn't noticed. But, he says, "God had seen me" (37).

Kevin resumes by describing how his relationship with Trish developed into a sexual thing, but they didn't talk about much and she, like Davy, wanted "more than the world had to give them" (*PA*, 38). One day when Trish is in college at NCAD, Clare and Kevin go to the supermarket together, which in Kevin's mind is like being married. As he remembers it, "she turned at one point and put her hand on my belly while we were looking at frozen pizzas. And for ages we couldn't move" (40).

Dermot is on the plane to Los Angeles, thinking that his wife knew he was lying when he said the company was making him travel alone. He drinks before the concert and at the concert also takes cocaine, which sends him into a paranoid fit. O'Hagan's wife finds him in a field and takes him to a party. But he blacks out, and the next thing he knows he is looking at a woman's breast implants while he is talking to his wife on the phone on the morning of St Patrick's Day. Imagining the family scene back in Ireland, he feels intense conflict and hurries off the phone with Mary. After drifting off again, he awakens to O'Hagan standing before him saying they confused him with someone of the same name, and he had better not sue (to retain his job or gain compensation) because they have good lawyers. In order to make a smoother exit, O'Hagan mentions that his mother, who had died a few months before, asked to have a photo of herself sent to a man who used to be their neighbour. But the past is over, he says, which echoes in Dermot's mind.

Joe explains that men of his generation don't know much about domestic things, so when they found a cyst on Liz's ovary, he needed to take the kids to Aunt Carmel in Baldoyle. Liz was holding up well at the hospital, so he was home when Marion came over with dinner for him. She also washed the dishes and said to call her if he needed anything else. After Marion returns home, Joe feels caught between guilt and desire: "I was afraid of my life that I'd be punished somehow by Liz's operation going awry in some way or that God was telling me he was taking her away because I was really supposed to be with somebody else" (*PA*, 48). That night he visits

Tommy and Marion's house for a nightcap. They attend to their child, who has a small fever, leaving Joe alone in the living room, where he spots a black and white picture of Marion as a young girl. In his mind, it shows her "between innocence and a dawning mischief" (49), and he starts to put it in his pocket when she returns, offering the picture to him. But he says he is only cleaning it and returns home, knowing he is afraid to take it "because I didn't know why I wanted it" (50).

The party at Kevin's is so wild that guards and an ambulance arrive. Speedy locks himself in the toilet, boys are urinating in the garden, and some party-goers have found Davy's homebrew. A girl falls down the stairs, and couples infiltrate Kevin's and Clare's bedrooms. Then a fight erupts between one of Clare's old boyfriends and Declan. When Trish discovers she is snogging another guy, not Kevin, she kicks the interloper in the face. "It was that type of atmosphere", Kevin summarises (*PA*, 52). Impromptu football games form, and someone claims Paul McCartney is there. When the guards try to arrest Davy, Clare defends him as mentally ill. Clare and Kevin decide to take a long walk, to Ringsend, Sandymount, Booterstown, Blackrock, Monkstown, and out to the harbour in Dun Laoghaire. Finally, with only the sea facing them, they have to turn back.

Kevin then changes scenes abruptly. He is back home with his parents and sisters. But he's happy; the room is tidy, and he has slept for fifteen hours. Clare comes by for tea, saying she is going crazy at her folks, but she will return to Declan and the band, Kevin is sure. He and she could not talk properly about themselves; they were afraid of trusting that they found each other so easily, he reflects. A few weeks later, his granny dies, and he remembers watching his granddad holding the beads she had gotten at Lourdes. That's when he developed the idea that there aren't souls for everyone in the world. Just one for those who go with the flow and one for the fighters. And some share a soul. He has been seeing

Trish down in Parliament Street, and he has "more than just a sneaky suspicion that if she was going to fight for me, that I was going to go with the flow" (*PA*, 55). He is going to settle for life without Clare.

Dermot summarises his situation after the LA debacle as "I felt like a man who'd been shot up into the air and all the lads with the nets had fucked off" (*PA*, 56). When he gets home and tells Mary about the mistake, she laughs as Colm, his son, runs his small finger across his father's beard. Despite all his mischief, his domestic life is returning feelingly. Then his wife tells him that she chose him "because you were alone in the world. And I knew you probably would be for the rest of your life and I decided that I was going to be your friend" (58). She adds that she knows he isn't attracted to her much any more, but he will always need someone to care for him and she always will. In Dermot's mind, he could see the three of them from above, her hand on the back of his head and his head falling slowly into her lap.

At Tighe's bar with Jackie Fennel and Mary Larkin, Joe has the picture in his pocket and is wondering why Marion Ross had it sent to him. He reflects that he might have been more balanced if he had known her better. But mostly it wasn't in him to have battled to make it happen. Once you make a decision, your life runs its course. Back at the home, Joe goes to his room to retire. He is too tired to finish his cowboy book, so he lies back with Marion's photograph in one hand and Liz's rosary beads from Lourdes in the other, tired of regret, he says, and whacked out from worry. He puts the two objects on his chest, "And I did what any Christian would do. I turned out the light and I went to sleep" (*PA*, 61).

In the stage directions to *Port Authority*, Conor McPherson is explicit that this play, like most of his others, requires a deconstruction of the illusion of the theatre. "The play is set in the theatre", he instructs producers and directors (*PA*, 7). But the realism of its setting is complemented by the uncertainties in the relationships. References to The Bangers in the stories by Kevin and Dermot link the two speakers in the most general way. A bit more personally, O'Hagan's mention of his mother's sending along a picture to the old people's home suggests that he could be the son of Marion, the woman Joe loves from afar. With a bit more stretching, the beads which Joe holds at the end of his narrative could identify him as the grandfather of Kevin, if the beads are the same ones his grandmother brought back from Lourdes. Such possible connections are never clarified; "The narrative links between the tales are tenuous. What matters is that the three men, while representing different facets of Ireland, all occupy the same emotional wasteland. Kevin's world is that of half-assed pub bands, Dermot moves in the shiny milieu of the Emerald Tiger and Joe faces his end in a nice, nun-run home" (Billington, 2001: par. 3). Written just a few months before *Come On Over*, *Port Authority* is just one step from the abstract impressionism of that play.

The resonance in *Port Authority* begins with the title. Like the bus station in New York City, the setting is a transitory meeting place, energised but also fleeting. A port authority, in the visual language of the play, is also a metaphor for the theatre itself, which McPherson carefully recreates. Both the New York building and the theatre offer momentary revelation, but they aren't domestic, peaceful places. More broadly, the title suggests a world in which authority itself is not stable; once the rules of public life have been made contingent and relative, they become portable. The intimate world is adrift, free from absolutes but carrying a heavier burden of loneliness. In this recent play, McPherson has moved far from the literalness of *Rum and Vodka*, the literariness of *This Lime Tree Bower*, and the minimalism of *The Weir*. The title of *Port Authority* suggests the subject is less a specific person or private moment than a general condition. The play is written against the background of freedom and isolation. The dark side of mischief is palpable in *Port Authority*.

As Michael Billington has identified, the play is about "missed opportunities" (2001: par. 1). These three men, while essentially alone on stage, are aware of each other and share their common inability to establish stable and sustaining relationships with women. Kevin loses his "soul mate" because of his inability to separate healthily from parents and integrate his emotions and sexuality. His fragmented life is reflected in his need to be passive in the face of a sexually aggressive woman and his lack of the courage necessary to pursue more complete intimacy with Clare. Dermot, living on the middle ground, is obsessed with bourgeois values and shallow relationships. More to the point, he is a perpetual child in search of a mother who will understand and protect him. And Joe, while supported by a belief system which helps him die like a Christian, is unable to square his ethical abstractions with effective action.

Port Authority is about Irish men who are "congenitally clumsy in dealing with affection" and consequently treat "women as either idolised Madonnas or base sex objects" (Billington, 2001: par. 3). But their stories indicate their desire to move beyond such polarities toward courageously pursuing loving attachment or learning that intimacy is more than sex. The repeated image of women-as-Madonna, in the rosary carried by Joe or Dermot cradled in Mary's lap, is not just male dependency. It is a vision of compassion and comfort that is the beginning of ethical understanding. Once again, McPherson is returning to the theme of unconditional acceptance as an antidote to the guilt that haunts his characters. These men need to distance themselves from the terror of worthlessness by finding a peace which absorbs their feelings of emptiness. They reimagine the Madonna, either literally or in their relationships with women, because of their longing for friendship and mutual understanding which triumph over licence.

The most resonant image in *Port Authority* is the sea as a place of impossibility, a valuable boundary between mischief and morality. Previous characters either stay in limbo or talk themselves into or out of various purgatories. But the flight of Clare and Kevin ends at the water's edge; with imagery remarkably similar to that in Joe's background at the end of *Saltwater*, this couple find themselves at the point where escape and evasion are no longer available: "We were running out of land to walk on. It was just miles and miles of sea. There was just nowhere left to go anymore. Except just sort of towards each other for a while" (*PA*, 53). No longer able to be merely playful, perverse, or suggestive, they have to act or choose not to act. In this case, Clare and Kevin don't trust the ease with which they found each other; paralysis keeps them from love, as Kevin sees it, and so they are only together "for a while". Nevertheless, choice and responsibility have arrived in McPherson's imaginative world because the cycle of guilt/mischief/destruction has become limited. Characters who either drifted, like Joe, or were driven by secret dependencies, like Dermot, are awakening to the decisions which reveal their true natures. They are free to become moral beings, not just mischief-makers.

In the process, the view of mischief changes. In the early works, it is typically a form of debauchery, a tendency to be perverse, exploitative and often violent. The intent of the monologue is confession mixed with self-explanation, and sometimes defence. With *The Weir*, this approach evolves into the struggle between these impulses and the desire to create a reasonable life, which traces an ethical arc. It is not so much that McPherson or his characters have a moral agenda. It is the recognition that behaviour is ethics and that in order to expect love, one must learn how to act lovingly in the world. It is the moral utilitarianism that he defended in his master's thesis (*LCAPR*, 164–65). The negative pole is established in *Dublin Carol*, where mischief must be checked or it will become self-deluding and alienating to the rebel and those who care for him. Then, in *Port Authority*, McPherson reminds himself and his audience that mischief can be a source of positive energy. Kevin's perversity is less consequential than his inability to embrace intimacy. And Joe could not escape to pursue risky love. If mischief brings good lovers together, it is healthy; but if mischief is an expression of fear, then it encourages alienation.

Formally, the difference is established by McPherson's finding new possibilities in the monologue. The early monologues were too fast-paced and slick to attend to such abstractions as the human condition. The speakers in *Rum and Vodka*, *The Good Thief*, and even *St Nicholas*, seduce the audience away from the larger contexts for their words and actions. *Port Authority* is more like *This Lime Tree Bower* and *Saltwater* in its focus on the loneliness of the contemporary Irish male. But in between is also the destructive nature of John's desire to justify himself in *Dublin Carol*, which McPherson consciously foreshortens in recognition of the pathology in such talk. Having revealed the darkness in its own dance, the monologue in *Port Authority* can no longer be a free ride for the narrators. The paralysis of their will and the lack of substance in their human contacts have replaced their own stories as the subject of these monologues. Rather than celebrate the unprecedented possibilities for a new generation of Irish males, as had the earlier monologues, this play reveals the loneliness which haunts such empty speakers.

Come On Over

Conor McPherson's most recent play premiered as one of three in an evening of one-acts at the Gate Theatre, Dublin. The other plays were *The Yalta Game*, Brian Friel's adaptation of a Chekhov short story, and *White Horses* by Neil Jordan. The three short plays opened on Tuesday, 2 October 2001, and ran until 17 November. *Come On Over* was directed by the author, with set design by Eileen Diss, costuming by Dany Everett, and lighting design by Mick Hughes. It featured Dearbhla Molloy and Jim Norton.

In McPherson's production of *Come On Over*, the main characters are preceded onto the stage by four children, who play flutes before and after the play. The two speakers, Matthew and Margaret, enter wearing "plain clothes and hoods", which "should look like mass-produced sacking and have neat holes for the eyes and mouth". "They sit and regard the audience", to whom their initial words are addressed (*COO*, 2).

Matthew begins by saying he arrived at Margaret's and joined her in watering the tomato plants. He confesses that he found Margaret old-looking and explains that he had spent the previous two months recovering "from an experience [. . .] in Africa" which required medication in Belgium (*COO*, 3). And Father Sebarus held an A4 envelope, which would change Matthew "even further than I'd already gone. Maybe even back to what I had been" (3).

Margaret adds that she left that scene because she started to cry. She also thought him old. But the tomatoes reminded her of an October thirty years before, when they were lovers walking in a rose garden, her hand clasping his in the pocket of his coat. She had worn a skirt, she says, in hopes he would touch her, but she already sensed that he was lost to her.

Matthew then explains that the envelope he received from Father Sebarus while recovering in Belgium contained photographs of a thirteen- or fourteen-year-old girl whose body had been discovered while workers were relocating a graveyard at St Monica's, Matthew's home parish. The corpse was four hundred years old and almost perfectly preserved, with the girl surrounded by blue flowers.

Margaret adds that Matthew became a Jesuit, a rational, scientific man who travelled over the world investigating supposed miracles. She had been shocked when he decided to pursue the cloth, though she thought him courageous and supported him, adding, "I don't think I need to tell you that it broke my heart" (*COO*, 5).

Matthew says that in the "deadly quiet" that night he resorted to his "procedure" of getting some toilet roll and "crying my eyes out, 'til I thought I couldn't breathe" (*COO*, 5). He felt better in the morning, but now feels the experience was somehow wrong: "it's not good for a man to lie there all night terrified. It's not right" (6).

Margaret says she had a full Irish breakfast ready when Matthew came down, neat and shaven but only able to smoke Silk Cut reds and drink tea. She retired to the drawing room, leaving him with his leg shaking under the table, the old clock ticking, and his chair scratching "on the kitchen floor like God himself had come to save him" (6).

The church, Matthew adds, was so cold they could see their breaths as a chap from UCD talked on a phone and a woman from Trinity supervised students taking samples. He was detached, mesmerised by the beautiful body of the child, which inspired him against his will because, as he admits, he had lost his faith a long time before. With "something in me begging to be free", Matthew had to retreat after Father Sebarus gave him a light "because if I didn't I was going to turn and smash his face in" (*COO*, 7).

Margaret switches the scene to Galway, where her husband, Patrick, died from leukaemia. He was a big man, she says, with "fingers like potatoes", but had withered to skin and bone. She wanted to crawl under the covers with him at the end and was holding his hand when "he went" (*COO*, 7). After Nuala, their daughter, finished at UCG and began her travels, Margaret also took care of Patrick's father, but he was no bother. During those times, she would write to Matthew, feeling he needed kind words, and would take down "the net curtains to wash them. I don't know why. Like a stupid candle in the bloody window" (8).

On the starry night Matthew returned to the chapel, a little sacristan turned on the lights so that Matthew could pray.
Obsessed with the corpse, he felt she had come through time
to relieve his loneliness. He wanted to see her again, but the
body had already been packed in a thermal case and sent to
Dublin. Suddenly he folds his arms on stage and admits, incongruously, that he is a racist who believes that blacks and
whites "age differently" (*COO*, 8).

Margaret then confesses she would hold Matthew's V-
neck sweaters to her face, feeling she was sucking him in
through her nose, as the tops of her legs leaned against the
bed. She also used to dance with the Pioneers in Jamestown,
leaning with her nose against the shoulder of a seventy-year-
old bachelor and smelling the turf and cigarettes.

Matthew interrupts her by declaring he was "temporarily
lost" (*COO*, 9). Margaret tells him to stop, but then she tells
him to go on, that she is sorry. The interchange stops briefly
as Matthew tells the audience that something dreadful happened to him, which again leads to an interjection from Margaret, followed by another apology. Matthew continues that
while in Africa he visited an Englishman, suspected by a nurse
of abusing a young girl named Patience. Then he stops, telling
Margaret, "We don't even have time for this!" She encourages him to go on, adding, "Because I have things to say" (10).
Matthew then takes tablets from his pocket, drops them, and
fumbles with them as he continues.

He says that after thirty years of reflection, he discovered
that the tablets always fall to the ground because it is God's
will. He admits that he hasn't always been in his "right mind",
but this conclusion about causality gave him the courage to
confront the Englishman, who "went pale, staring at his car-
pet and his pool" (*COO*, 11). Matthew first pitied the man and
then felt the beginning of a blinding migraine as he passed Patience on the return to his home. He could only think of getting into a dark room and putting a cold cloth on his head.

Awakened in the night, he turned the light on and saw Patience standing before him, having let herself in with a key. He pulled the covers back, telling himself for the tenth time "this'd be the last time". She attacked him with a knife, causing him to lose his left eye and half his nose. He adds that he was saved because the knife became embedded between his teeth, so "She couldn't get it out again" (12).

Margaret begins to explain that he was going to Dublin the morning after visiting her. Matthew tries to interrupt her by asking "What are you doing?" (*COO*, 12). But she continues by saying she asked him to stay and began to reminisce about their last day together when young. This time Matthew joins her, adding that he corrected her memory, saying that it couldn't have been St Brigid's Day, which is in the spring, not October. She continues that he came to her bedroom that night, that she rubbed his shoulder, put her arm around his tummy, and felt his erection against the inside of her arm. As she makes these confessions, Margaret takes off her hood, which Matthew tells her to replace. She continues her description, Matthew repeatedly imploring her to replace the mask. She adds that while he was rubbing himself against her left arm, she remembered this was the first erect penis she had touched (when they were young) and she wondered where else Matthew's had been. Once again he calls her name, trying to get her to stop (13). She says she was also thinking about how many Nuala had felt.

As Matthew calls her name again, asking her to put the hood back on, she laments the loss of Nuala and finally turns to Matthew, declaring, "You're no good. I'd take you in. I don't care about anything" (*COO*, 14). He responds by asking her not to do this to herself. She finally replaces her hood and explains that the body had started to decompose in Dublin. As Matthew returns to his religious explanations of the events, Margaret repeatedly protests with "No" (14). He says his greatest sin was not trusting God, who had sent the girl to forgive him and show him a miracle. In the printed version, Margaret responds by getting up, throwing her chair at him, and leaving. In the version staged at the Gate, she instead crosses to him and cradles him against her chest.

Come On Over is McPherson's most abstract play. Previous plays imitated the world outside the theatre and emphasised the directness of the communication between the character and the audience. Despite the violence in the stories and the prevarications in the telling, the dramas were concrete and driven by their own kinds of sincerity. In *Come On Over*, the story is the most familiar element in an environment made alien by the primitive music, placeless costumes, and dehumanising masks. Having discovered, as he says, the power of the actor's faces to establish empathy in the filming of *Saltwater*, McPherson denies such intimacy in his most recent production. Once the audience settles into such lack of personality, Margaret removes her mask and the characters wrestle over whether she should reveal herself so nakedly, both to Matthew and, more uncomfortably, to the audience. Where earlier works either accept the fourth wall or erase the usual conventions of civil discourse, this play relies on a mischievous triangle in which the audience is drawn into the game of appearances. The characters imagine the audience as a third player, one from whom information can be withheld, either through self-protection or coercion.

As McPherson suggests in the interview in this book, *Come On Over* is designed to explore the dialectic of expression/retention. It is not clear whether Margaret's desire to expose herself, through the details in her story and her unmasking, is a useful and healthy impulse. Certainly her words and actions help clarify for the audience the degree of sexual involvement between her and the priest. But her obsessive desire for him, her inability to create healthy boundaries for herself in this relationship, have also caused chronic dissatisfaction and frustrating fantasies that paralyse her. Matthew, on the other hand, has hidden many secrets in his pursuit of order and truth, continually confusing loneliness with emptiness. The play does not clarify whether any good would be gained by his unmasking. Even as Margaret brings the full story to light, he resorts to yet another abstract interpretation, trading his earlier rationalism for an equally distancing assertion of divine intervention. The characters live in a tormented state in which desire is not liberating and traditional boundaries are inadequate.

The phrasing in the title — *Come On Over* — parodies the lilt in a tourist board advert. Instead of a beautiful land of sweet people, the playwright gives a dark image of an Irish priest following the lead of the colonial English in acts of violation, in both Africa and Ireland. Since his attacks on Patience and his liaisons with Margaret are sexual, the word "come" also suggests the vernacular for orgasm, making this title, like *I Went Down*, sexually suggestive. The bawdiness is toned down here, made more allusive than explicit, because McPherson is not dramatising sexual politics as he was in the film; the play focuses instead on the split between the earthy and the divine implied in the words "on" versus "over". In *Come On Over*, McPherson places the physical next to the morally aspiring, with all the confusions and doubts that follow. While an over-emphasis on either the material or the spiritual leads to delusions or perversions, the writer sides with the existential realities of Margaret, her goodness being the only source of potential redemption.

Most interesting are the two endings, both of which are designed to discomfort the audience. McPherson says he prefers to write organically, and yet only the written conclusion offers an emotional release from the dramatic tension between the characters. In that case, Margaret's attack is a personal response to Matthew's failure to love her either physically or emotionally. She finally releases her frustration and delivers a fit retribution that leaves them separated and their intimacy lost. In the staged version, the sudden comfort Margaret offers Matthew, despite his repeated betrayals, alienates the viewers by reversing the dramatic trajectory of *Come On Over*, redirecting the story to a forced and thus maddening closure. Together, however, the endings suggest the emotional dilemma of McPherson's males when confronted with emotionally active women. Hopefully the men will be supported and loved, even if they drift into a fog, as Matthew does in *Come On Over*. But they also might be attacked and abandoned. Either way, their emptiness can only be filled by the grace, in the sense of undeserved love, of a woman. Incapable of nurturing themselves, the men become the objects of luck and female initiative.

Matthew's confusion is typical of the McPherson males. Caught between off-putting anger and the clumsy pursuit of pleasurable ethics, they have difficulty imagining authentic choice and responsible freedom. Continually reacting to repressive authority or the absence of useful principles, they either turn their anger outward, as in the case of his early monologists, or inward as with his more recent characters. There is more hope in *Dublin Carol* and *Port Authority* because the characters imagine usable boundaries. However, *Come On Over* is more troubling than even the early plays because its dialogue and care are marked by inauthenticity; boundaries are either obliterated or have hardened into barriers which alienate the spiritual from the physical. In the process, romance is equated with obsession and choice has retreated in the face of unrelieved need and unfulfilled desire.

Nevertheless, these recent plays make clear that McPherson's mischievous characters and theatrical trips do not simply serve licence, as some critics have written. Even in his earliest work, but more insistently and rhetorically in his last plays (and films), his characters reach clear and present moments which require them to choose. While not exactly epiphanies, because the characters do not usually see themselves or the world anew, these moments are nevertheless defining, even for the least reflective and most compulsive ones. As they turn back from the brink, from the time and place of impossibility, the most reasonable and connected of the McPherson characters consider their first steps toward responsibility — away from death and into empathy and compassion. Some accept their limitations and need for others. Others also start to care for themselves and their attachments.

The audiences are invited to share those decisive moments and take personal notes about the modern and very human conflict between thoughtless repression and pure acting out. McPherson, a student of ethics, suggests that there is a moral imperative even among the infinite novelties and mysteries of contemporary life. His mischievous characters and perverse dramas do not finally tell self-defining and liberationist stories. As he says, he has no personal or political agenda about how and where these characters should find themselves between the poles of rebellion and responsibility. But McPherson invites his spectators to awaken to such dilemmas. If they are willing to assume the role of observing egos, they will learn to play at both mischief and morality.

Chapter Six

Mischief and Morality

In an article in the London *Sunday Times*, Conor McPherson described the evolution of his dramatic style:

> I started out trying to copy David Mamet, having businessmen in their shirtsleeves shouting at each other. I liked that argumentative stuff because you could write it quickly. After a while I wanted to get to the heart of characters rather than just have that showy surface affair. So I started to write characters from the inside out by using monologues. (Heaney, 1999: 21)

The monologue, realised in a variety of dramatic forms, freed McPherson to use resonant details, the rhythms of idiomatic language and multiple settings, a combination which he describes as cinematic writing:

> In all my work, one of the common things, I think, is that it's pure exposition. There's very little mystery. As soon as you see the characters, they're telling you who they are. And, I suppose, cinema is pure exposition, because you see everything. The plays, which are primarily monologues, do that as well. You describe everything, every detail. It's almost like an extended shotlist. (Duane, 1997: 15)

As director, he then asks his actors to refrain from acting out emotions and situations which cloud the narration. In his words, he wants his players to "trust the story to do the work" (McPherson, "Author's Note" to *TLTB*, 5).

But this emphasis on storytelling is not as simple as some critics have argued. It is not enough to say Conor McPherson has inherited what William Trevor calls the "instinctive" Irish "delight in stories" which "serve both as entertainment and as a form of communication" (1989: xv, ix). Instead of revelling in the stories themselves, McPherson uses the monologue to experiment with the communication between the actor-playing-a-character and "the audience" which "becomes the other character" (Renner, 1998: 62). In the process:

> a past personal ordeal is converted into a kind of present public ordeal. That is, a previous test of character, one which often reflects unfavourably on the speaker, becomes the basis for a story which, however fantastic, through the symbiosis of telling and listening redeems the speaker. Even as his misfits reveal themselves as creatures of conscience, guilt, and regret, their storytelling restores to them a measure of lost innocence that can be had by no other means. (Cummings, 2000: 311–12)

While communication is redemptive for his characters, McPherson stops short of justifying their views or actions. His theatre is not a simple celebration of single voices. While often quite mesmerising, his storytelling is also disingenuous, recognising at every moment that "all theatre deals with illusion, implicitly or explicitly". Personally "fascinated by questions of performance", McPherson repeatedly draws attention to the physical theatre and the presence of the audience. He trains his actors to play with the reality that "you know they're actors and they're trying to convince you otherwise, and you are being seduced and lied to and you have to go with that" (McKenzie, 2001a: par. 5). The illusory is

> a way of drawing attention to the psychology of story-telling. When regarded collectively, his body of work demonstrates a self-consciousness about the mechanics of McPherson's craft that adds a meta-narrative dimension to his tall tales. They become, in part, stories about storytelling. (Cummings, 2000: 306)

The mischief is not just in the raving characters. It is in the telling as well, though written by a dramatist responsible enough to remind his viewers of the magic he is performing.

Equally as subject to misinterpretation as his art of storytelling is the nature of Conor McPherson's Irishness. To critics outside Ireland, who see it as "the place of isms: Catholicism, lyricism, colloquialism, alcoholism", McPherson's home place requires that he be artless: "He has a fine ear for the lilt and eccentricities of Irish speech, and his characters are observed with great respect and high colour. But he lacks a way of giving them a play to play with" (Kanfer, 1999: 22). If the critic feels he is at the centre of the universe, in, say, New York City, he may condescend and whine at the same time: "How much more inundation by booze and blarney can our woozy heads withstand?" In the words of such self-absorbed reviewers, *The Weir* seems merely an example of "a perennial fascination with the brogue" and "aromatic Hibernian cadences" (Simon, 1999a: 84). In the minds of such reviewers, *The Weir* lacks sophistication because, being Irish, it necessarily indulges in the "picturesque" and "Hibernian whimsy" (Brustein, 1999: 33). Such are the racist tendencies of ethnocentric criticism.

His Irishness can be equally misunderstood by critics who respect Irish playwrights. Being from Ireland, McPherson must write political allegory, these interpreters conclude; to them, *This Lime Tree Bower* is "inescapably set against a backdrop of

the conflict in the North" or *The Weir* is "a requiem for Ireland" of old and *Dublin Carol* an anthem for new Ireland
(McPherson, 1998b: 40; McPherson, 1999g: par. 3, 21). Or
they lump McPherson with Martin McDonagh, concluding that
they both mourn a contemporary Irish "society in which stories make less and less sense" (O'Toole, 1998: 19). Since
McPherson is Irish, these writers assume, his goal as an artist
must be "to strip 'Irishness' of its nationalistic and romantic
myths and see what is left" (Riding, 1997: AR1). To correct
such assumptions, McPherson has reminded readers that his
generation experienced "confused detachment from the violence in Ireland", feeling "helplessness or impotence in the
face of so much bitterness". About Irish patriots, he wonders,

> Do we dwell on the great injustices they suffered and
> become increasingly upset about something we can
> never really make right? Or do we simply embrace the
> future they've secured for us? Which is the best way
> to honour them? (McPherson, 1998b: 40–41)

In order to understand his particular brand of Irish writing, he suggests that audiences look to his style and vision,
not just the details place and history have given him:

> I think that Ireland figures importantly principally as a
> setting, and of course the setting influences the con-
> cepts and themes . . . but Ireland is not the most fun-
> damental, absolute idea. I mean, I react to it to get
> material for my work but I mainly write about Ireland
> because I happen to live there. (McKenzie, 2001a:
> par. 7)

Although his work should always be distinguished from theirs,
McPherson is a member of "a third wave of twentieth-century
Irish theatre", which includes Martin McDonagh, Sebastian
Barry, Marina Carr and Frank McGuinness. These writers

> don't see being Irish as either something that has to
> be self-consciously embraced (as Synge did) or as
> something to be avoided at all costs (as Beckett did,
> going so far as to write in French). They have, in a
> sense, nothing to prove, at least as far as their place in
> Irish culture and society is concerned. There's a kind
> of simple confidence in their work that comes from
> being able to take for granted the idea that "Irish" is
> an adjective that covers a multitude of differences.
> (O'Toole, 1998: 17)

It is as a personal writer, not a debunker, that Conor McPherson has "taken Irish drama away from its habitual obsessions with nationality, history and identity" (Kilroy, 2000: 5).

What remains Irish, according to the playwright, is his interest in the emotional lives of his characters, without objectification or generalisation. This is what distinguishes, he feels, the tendencies in British and Irish drama. He considers Martin McDonagh in the British tradition, which is "about relationships within a kind of societal structure or hierarchy. They're interested in who has the power in an actual relationship, where Irish writers tend to write from the inside out" (O'Connell, 2000: 38). Or to put it another way, "British theatre tends to examine the outer structure of situations. Martin's stuff is, 'What's the effect of an oppressive area on people who seem to be mad to begin with?'" while "Irish work tends to deal with the inner life of a character, with very basic hopes and fears and the imaginative world" (Wolf, 1998a: AR8). In other words, Conor McPherson claims the Irish theatrical tradition of dramatising the subjective life of its characters, without impersonal, uncompassionate judgement. The best of Irish dramatic writing avoids, he says, the dehumanisation of art.

Many critics feel McPherson's own humanity is compromised when he writes, especially in the single monologues, about "shits and fuck-ups" obsessed with trouble-making. In this view, the "mischievous quality" of the play equates "getting out of a predicament" with "getting away with something, an indiscretion, a sin, a crime or just the obnoxious bravado of a drunk" (Cummings, 2000: 305). For these reviewers, it is worrisome that "The monologues derive their dramatic charge from the energies of transgression" (Renner, 1998: 63). In their opinion, McPherson has a "fascination for the drink-driven excesses of lad culture", motivated by the need "to prove the validity of the booze-and-birds lifestyle, which is routinely contrasted with anything pretentious or middle-class" (McCarthy, 2000a: 9). Other writers, more sympathetic to McPherson's achievement, answer that the narratives are the speakers' attempts to bring order to their otherwise "chaotic and troubling experience". The stories and plays become, variously, "a plea for sympathy, an act of expiation, an affirmation of sanity, an effort to conquer or seduce, or a confession" (Cummings, 2000: 311). McPherson's narrators are not, finally, freewheeling because "[c]asting judgement" on their "credibility" is essential to "a more general judgement" encouraged by the playwright (307).

It is crucial in McPherson's theatre that the speaker's words are judged without his character being condemned, no matter how mischievous his feelings and actions. His speakers need audiences who offer the players a vicarious expiation of guilt. As McPherson has asserted, "We all need to be redeemed, really. We're always offending God by fucking existing. I think we're brought up as children feeling like very bad people." For him "stories [. . .] help us try and make sense of the terrible guilt that we feel. We feel terribly ashamed of ourselves. We're afraid of ourselves, so we sort of project it out there" (Renner, 1998: 63). No matter what "misadventures overtake them and whatever ignominy or sorrow may come as a result, the fact of having a story and the act of telling it constitute a kind of redemption, a saving grace which imbues their profane lives with a touch of the sublime"

(Cummings, 2000: 303). Simple on the surface, McPherson's plays gain complexity by being designed as "profane confessionals" (Renner, 1998: 63).

The audiences are essential to such confessing because the antagonist in the plays is not immorality. It is loneliness, according to their author:

> I think all stories have a healing function, because what they say is that you're not alone. If a play or a production of a play works, what it does is it defines the community. Because at the beginning of the night everyone goes in and they're all separate people, and the actors are separate to the audience. But by the end of the night, if the thing has worked, everybody comes out feeling that they're all on the same team. You feel human, and that it's OK to be human. It's trying to give you a sympathetic view of people that you may even consider your enemies. (Kilroy, 2000: 5)

It takes more than a troubled narrator and a compelling story. Equally necessary is an audience which, like Brendan in *The Weir*, "sacrifices doubt to compassion and accepts the experience of the aggrieved as given", becoming in the process an instrument of healing (Cummings, 2000: 310).

The audience is also served by the passing sense of community designed into a McPherson play. In the background of each theatrical event is McPherson's recognition, gained in his studies as a philosophy student, of the "ambiguity of it all [. . .] we don't really know very much and [. . .] everybody is winging it" (Carty, 2000a: 2). But human consciousness instinctively rebels, the writer believes, against such uncertainty. Whatever their emotional or intellectual capacities, McPherson's characters seek meaningful order, inspired by reason and requiring, eventually, a degree of responsibility ("Author's Note" to *SN*, in *TWAOP*, 76). Even his highest flyers are conscience-stricken, play at ethics, or attempt to reason themselves toward some degree of peace. Being instinctively attracted to "the complexity of ethical choice", to "morality and its difficulty", the audience is invited to become observing egos in the dramas (Kilroy, 2000: 5). Even his wildest stories are games "played against the grain of ethics" which allow the observers to "to explore the consequences without having to actually take them" and, hopefully, "work out the good or the bad of a situation" for themselves (Renner, 1998: 62; Nowlan, 2001: par. 5). McPherson's theatre of mischief is designed to stimulate the moral imagination of his audience, without endorsing any specific morality itself.

The lure of irresponsibility needs to be played off against the humanising need to reflect, to engage reason, because of the absence of potent benign authority in his work. Sometimes life is unstable because the characters inhabit the violent landscapes of gangsterism and intrigue. At other times, McPherson's characters are driven by spellbinding moments of self-assertion, both angry and comic. Consequently, they observe loving connections, like those in healthy families, as voyeurs rather than committed partners. Even when they are married with children, as in *Rum and Vodka*, they flee the routines of domesticity. While the images and rituals of religious experience haunt them, McPherson's men typically ridicule, reject, or aimlessly drift from religious piety. Pleasure, not received morality, is their most potent source of energy and human interchange in a world in which the old rules no longer apply.

But pleasure is not simple for these characters. Even the most explosive of them is instinctively drawn to the order offered by reasoned responses to such troubling environments. Driven by a basic desire for the control and peace found in calculating one's situation, needs and expectations, McPherson's people stumble, with varying degrees of sweet success and comic failure, toward ethics and personal morality. Even if not capable of love, the characters become mesmerised by images of mutuality. They sense their creator's assertion that affection is given in the hope, or at least the increased chance, that it will be returned. McPherson's theatre is not a playground for raunchy, childish men, though they are often the protagonists of his work. It is a stage constructed on the ethical/moral boundary, where his men and women are given the opportunity to turn back toward others. Meanwhile, his mischievous plays invite audiences to practise compassion and, hopefully, imagine their own reasonable conclusions.

The result is a surprisingly conservative aesthetic. As Fintan O'Toole has correctly identified, McPherson is a member of that 1990s generation of Irish dramatists who, despite "their playfulness", leave behind "the theatrical avant-garde". Most obviously, Conor McPherson rejects the emphasis on the "physical" and the "grammar of the electronic media" of post-modern materialism. While employing more "literary language" than some of his contemporaries, the poetry in his plays is inspired by transparent colloquialisms and arresting imagery, not verbal artifice. There is a return to traditional narrative, though the "drive" is not always tightly structured. The obsessive talk frees his characters to wander wherever the human voice and imagination take them; the stories sometimes seem driven, sometimes desultory (O'Toole, 1998: 19; O'Toole, 2000: par. 8, 10, 15). Finally, even more than his emphasis on storytelling, McPherson's most conservative "virtue" is his justification of reason and a sense of community between the actor/character and the audience.

Such an approach to writing is not exactly psychological realism, though the history of the individual psyche has interested him in his most recent plays, beginning with *Dublin Carol*. His sensibility is haunted by Christian, specifically Catholic, myth and imagery. Thus he is not as close to O'Casey or Beckett as some have argued, despite the fact that he has filmed *Endgame*. His taste for the comic haunting of the modern, now post-modern, worldview by the ideal of community is closer to that of James Joyce. Having lost the moorings of received values and divine injunctions, his men are, as he says, "slightly hysterical" over the possibility of love. So they idealise women as "possibility embodied", "the chance to be happy" (White, 1998: par. 7) with an almost religious fervour. Especially in *Port Authority* and *Come On Over*, the Virgin Mary appears as a symbol of compassion in the face of the loneliness and self-destructive tendencies of many of the characters. Such a sense of unconditional acceptance and compassion is the only solace in the face of isolation, meaninglessness, and death.

Conor McPherson is a new kind of Irish exile. As much as Joyce, Beckett or Edna O'Brien, his work is specifically Irish. While they left Ireland — sooner or later — to gain a useful distance from their subject, McPherson works both at home and away. As Paddy Breathnach has explained with insight and humour, in working on *I Went Down*, the writer revealed himself as not just a Dublin writer but specifically a north Dublin writer. Nevertheless, Irish audiences have not always received his plays with open arms; the obscenity, betrayal of traditional dramatic form, and lack of closure have apparently estranged some Irish theatregoers, despite the success of his ensemble work in his homeland. In contrast, in England the messiness of his organic dramas is welcomed as a sign of the experimentalist nature of his work. And in the United States, once reviewers have gotten beyond their own stereotypic responses to Irish writing, McPherson is accepted as a comic playwright with a personal vision.

McPherson has responded to such partial exiling with some irritation and a great deal of flexibility. Without a conscious design, he has established a workable pattern for the short term. As he writes and produces new plays, he continues to enjoy the support of English theatre audiences. Dublin remains a secondary venue because he receives stronger financial and critical support in London. As his plays travel across the Atlantic to America, McPherson intends to follow them as a director, at least for their initial productions, in order to minimise revisions; he wants to assert the control more available to playwrights than screenwriters (Carty, 2000a: 2). When in Dublin, his friendship with writers like Cóilín O'Connor and Eugene O'Brien leads him back to the stage as director. Film also offers him new prospects; having made peace with the hassles of film production, he continues his collaborations with Paddy Breathnach, Robert Walpole, and Neil Jordan. Believing successful writers should take more risks in their maturity, Conor McPherson imagines a lot of mischief in his future, both in his dramas and the ways they are staged.

Appendix

An Interview with Conor McPherson

The following interview was recorded in two sessions. The first was late in the afternoon on Friday, 7 June 2001, at the Irish Film Centre, Temple Bar, Dublin. It lasted nearly two hours. The second was at the Grooms Bar, in Cassidys Hotel, across from the Gate Theatre, O'Connell Street, on Saturday, 10 November of the same year. It lasted an hour. Both times the author was initially a bit reserved, though concerned that our time together would be comfortable. He made sure we found quiet places and were not interrupted. And he paid for coffee on both occasions. Once the conversations began, he often averted his eyes, seemingly in thoughtful reflection, until a subject gripped his imagination and emotions. Then he became animated, focused, and often humorous in his responses.

Gerald Wood: Do ideas come to you as dialogue? Or characters? Or situations?

Conor McPherson: I just kind of see it. I see the story like a film. If it's too big a scope (if it's not in a room, like *Dublin Carol*, or in a pub, like *The Weir*), I am attracted to the monologue, which allows the story to breathe — in the theatrical sense — as the character tells it. Or I make it as a film.

GW: And then you add compelling and resonant voices.

CMcP: I try to get the characters to say something believable, believable because of some lived experience of my own. What they are talking about is moving from detail to detail, so I like those details to come organically.

GW: You try to make it as real as possible, and then something else is going on subconsciously.

CMcP: That's it. Like describing someone walking up some steps and deciding to sit down . . . on some stone steps. You just keep it very simple so people can relate to it. At the same time it seems to be a little picture of mortality or something. And after a while, when it is all mounted up, it is a barrage of experience.

GW: Describe, if you would, your writing process.

CMcP: I've written in all kinds of different ways, actually, even with a computer, but mostly just by scribbling. I tend to not spend a whole lot of time physically writing. I write in very short bursts, usually for about an hour. But in those bursts it is very clear what's going to happen, what the next bit is going to be. When I have a draft, I type it on an ordinary electric typewriter. That's it. I send it off.

GW: Is there a lot of stuff going on in your head between those bursts?

CMcP: Oh, yeah, that's what I'm always doing. I'm not the sort of person who sits down in front of a blank piece of paper and says, "Now what am I going to write about?" I learned a long time ago that the best things happen when you have an idea and you just leave it settle in your head, not sure what's going to happen next. And then the next day it seems very clear. If it starts getting hard, I just stop.

GW: When does the revision start?

CMcP: I tend to set up the production first. When I get into rehearsal, I work with the actors. As soon as actors start saying what I have written, I see how much of it I don't need. I just know when an actor's doing something much more naturally than what I've written. If I've got good judgement, and I hope I do, I am going to throw out my precious thing, my precious joke, whatever it is, which no one is getting. Good actors don't need to say, "I was boring, blah-blah-blah, and my parents were like this." They just imbue something with a life and personality, even while just sitting in a chair. If things are left unsaid, you wonder about them more just as you wonder about real people.

GW: So you collaborate with the actors in order to edit — to find the redundant or dead places in your writing.

CMcP: That's it. When I finish that process, then I say that is the finished script. However, if the actors have a problem with a piece, a section or whatever, I think it is important that they trust me, too. I've been very lucky with actors, who will trust my judgement and finally admit, "I don't know why this works."

GW: So revision focuses more on language than characterisation. Or do you talk about motive?

CMcP: I don't like to do that because the characters are quite simple . . . and yet complex at the same time. In *Come On Over*, I said to Dearbhla Molloy, "I know this is frustrating. But basically she is a good person." I know that sounds very glib, but it's hugely complex. What does "good" mean? It means she subjugates her own needs, sees more of her responsibility to others rather than herself. She's nice and wants to do the right thing. And Dearbhla trusted me with that. At the end of the process she said, "Yeah, it's like poetry. Each line in isolation doesn't mean an awful lot. But you put the whole thing together and it just makes sense. You need it all."

GW: So you give general instructions about the character, but you don't get too much into motive or analysis.

CMcP: I like to keep it general, very, very general. I know the actors are very intelligent and are going to pick things to hang onto, the little benchmarks that give them clues to the character. Then weeks later, they will have a whole story to say about the character: "I think she was from this place. I think she went to this kind of school. I think her relationship with her parents was like this." If you do another production with a different actress, she will have a completely different interpretation. And that's fine.

GW: And because your plays are minimal, you don't have to think much about positioning or actions on the stage.

CMcP: Well, I do have to think about it because I have to say, "Why aren't they moving?" You see people walking all around in a Tennessee Williams play. They are pouring themselves a drink, sitting down, going up to a window. But people don't walk around when they are having an interesting conversation. They get close and talk. Unless they are very uncomfortable and want to put the kettle on because they are uncomfortable.

GW: So you ask yourself what the characters would do in real life.

CMcP: I do. The characters in the monologues have no problem talking to the audience. Otherwise, they wouldn't do it. So, why move? This is where they want to be — on the stage.

GW: There seems to be more movement in *Dublin Carol* than in your other plays.

CMcP: There is. There's a lot of displacement. People are doing things because they are uncomfortable, trying to get out of the conversation. But that's a naturalistic kind of play.

GW: You have said that your early writing was influenced by David Mamet's work.

CMcP: I began by imitating him in the first play I wrote; I would've been about 18. It was a lunchtime one-act play that I did at the Drama Society at UCD. In those days *The Irish Times* used to review student plays, and I remember it got a very good review. But it was really like a Mamet play, businessmen in their shirtsleeves shouting at each other, just in Dublin, fast, furious, and a lot of swearing.

GW: That play won't be published?

CMcP: No. It really wasn't very good.

GW: You have also said that the monologue liberated you, helped you find your voice. How did you get from the Mamet-like plays to your experimentation with that form?

CMcP: I always had a knack for dialogue. Most dialogue in plays is fuelled by confrontation, and you can write pages and pages because your protagonists are repeating the same thing, not really getting anywhere. I found that restrictive; I wanted to tell smaller stories but in a bigger way. And I found that just by a single voice describing a situation, you could go to the moon, you could go anywhere. And the audience aren't stupid; their imagination is going to do the work. And audiences really, really liked it. Then I began to become interested in the theatre itself. When you have two or three actors pretending that the audience don't exist, there is that fourth wall and you're not really getting anything that you couldn't get better in cinema, TV, or a novel. What I thought people liked about the monologue was the titillation, the grey area, that we know this is an actor playing a character, and he knows that we know that he is, or she is, an actor. But we are all playing, a sort of a collusion. This game is being played, this kind of grown-up game. And it seemed to me so mischievous and exciting.

GW: *St Nicholas* seems to be a very important play. The narrator takes you places and really opens the storytelling up. And through him you began to say a few things rather than just being true to the voice itself.

CMcP: I think I was becoming more confident in working with direct address to the audience. And because I was confident about it, I was more playful, at least in the production I did, with the audience; we had a good time. We felt like it was supposed to be fun. And also thought-provoking.

GW: So the progression is from the single monologue to ones in which multiple speakers share a story, to now, in *Port Authority,* stories which overlap slightly but only in inconsequential ways.

CMcP: I think with *Port Authority* they do seem to know that the other people are there, at least in the production I've done. I think that each character somehow resonates off the others, but I really don't know how. I think it is just instinctive. And I put my hand on my heart and say I don't know if this works or why it works. It seems very disparate to the listeners, who kind of go "What is the concept?" It's a bit disingenuous. What do these people have in common? Well, really nothing, except they are in the same play. With *Come On Over*, I'm going further. Two characters talk in monologue. But then they begin talking to each other and it breaks down. I think that is a normal progression. It is like the thing is coming apart at its seams. So I don't think I am finished yet discovering what I want to do.

GW: How did being the director of *Port Authority* help with this experimentation?

CMcP: I was trying to give people the idea of a theatre. My first idea for the design was no set; whatever is there is just there. But actually theatres are very cluttered. They look like a fire station; there are ladders and fire extinguishers and tools on the walls . . . and pipes. It's actually very busy in the backstage area, which is not really what people think of as a theatre without a set. They would just think of it as an empty space. Actually, you have to generate an empty space, which was a quite interesting design problem.

GW: How did you continue such experimentation in *Come On Over*?

CMcP: The characters have bags over their heads, with just holes for their eyes and mouths. I have these little children, these girls, playing the recorders, with their uniforms, and I've got bags over their heads as well. The man and woman are describing these experiences, what happened to them, that turns into the issue of "Why do we have to wear these bags on our heads?" To me that is the whole point of the play: the notion of authority and what compels anyone to tell the truth. It's in this purgatorial kind of space really. Although the performances, even with these bags over their heads and the children playing the music, are very natural and the story is sort of ordinary. The whole drive of the play is poetic; it is trying to create an impression of an experience rather than a traditional play with a story. The play is really about why they have bags on their heads and who put them there. Visually it conjures images of being hostage, dead, or executed. Without the conventional successes I've had, I don't think I'd be doing this now. I wouldn't be allowed. For a first-time writer, director, the actors would convincingly ask, "Could we not have bags on our heads?" There is an element of trust which is earned. *Come On Over* confuses people because they want a neat engagement, a neat encounter between the audience and the actors. And they are used to me doing something more standard or at least accessible. And I think this one is accessible, but they need to just turn off their questioning hearts, just let it happen. I think it works.

GW: One reviewer said, "I'm not sure I'm informed enough to understand this" (Both laugh.)

CMcP: There's not an awful lot to understand. There really isn't. It's simple . . . and quite scary.

GW: So you were experimenting with masks, authenticity, hiding, and control.

CMcP: Yeah, that's it. It is more questioning than answering. In that way, it's more artistic, you know, but it works on all kinds of levels. It's also just a simple story. Just close your eyes and listen to the story. It's a nice story, a lovely story, I think. A very sad story.

GW: How does it feel as a writer when you are directing other people's work, for example, with Eugene O'Brien's *Eden* for theatre or Beckett's *Endgame* for film?

CMcP: I think I was very respectful of their work. When I direct my own work, I tend to change things if I sense an actor's discomfort. I'm always going into rehearsal with actors to see what they are going to bring. In *Saltwater*, for example, I was throwing away whole scenes and rewriting them ten minutes before we'd shoot. I had that freedom. I asked the Beckett estate if I could change one line of *Endgame*, which I thought was a translation thing where Beckett was letting himself down. Clov sees a small boy at the window, and Hamm says, "More complications." And he says, "Not an underplot, I hope." And I said to Edward Beckett, Beckett's nephew, "Really, this is what most people would understand as subplot, not underplot." And he said, "Well, you can't do anything about it now. Beckett's dead. Can't ask him." I wouldn't mess with Samuel Beckett's work. I just thought that if Beckett were alive, and I rang him up, I think he probably would say to go ahead, do you know? And Edward Beckett agreed with me that he probably would, but said, "The thing is — I can't." When I was directing Eugene's *Eden*, it was his first play, and I would suggest that he make cuts or take something from one part of the play and put it earlier for dramatic tension. He was very open to that. It was like the way I would work; I had the writer in the room with the actors so everything was agreed. So I suppose I probably prefer working with new work more than set texts.

GW: What would you say to anyone directing your work?

CMcP: As a general point, keep it very simple, as simple as possible, and it will be all right. Now I don't mean to say to go as far as not act, not think about character. What I suggest is just to tell the story.

GW: As you've said, trust the story to do the work.

CMcP: Exactly. If you embellish, or if you feel the need to embellish, it's quite distracting. And you're drawing attention to the acting, and consequently the actor looks weak. If the actor doesn't do very much, he or she looks very strong. It's very important that the storyteller is in charge. With *Port Authority*, the middle character, played by Stephen Brennan, often had a problem with the audience; he said, "I can't get a word in, the laughs are coming and I can't actually speak because it is too noisy." And it's tough, but my note to him was "Well, that's your problem. You've got to deal with it. You've got to stop them." (He laughs.) It's very, very difficult. The people have paid their money, and they are going to enjoy it whatever way they want. But a good actor will take charge.

GW: You have said that three-quarters of the people who saw *The Weir* interpreted the title differently than you do. I am particularly interested in *Dublin Carol*, *Port Authority*, and the renaming of *This Lime Tree Bower* as *Saltwater*. What did you have in mind with those titles?

CMcP: Titles are often the hardest part. I like to keep them short. *Saltwater* just seemed to resonate. Obviously no one had named a film *This Lime Tree Bower*, and I liked *Saltwater* because it seems to refer to something the audience might have seen before. With *Dublin Carol* you've got something that is also almost recognisable, like a Christmas Carol and the name of a city — Dublin. If you ask people if they've seen it, they go "I don't know; it sounds familiar." If you ask people if they've seen *Port Authority*, they go, "I've heard of Port Authority. It's a bus station in New York. Have I seen the play? I don't know." It's a bit above people's heads.

GW: So you are not sure it would resonate for Irish audiences.

CMcP: For me, it is taken from the bus station in New York. It is a place where disparate people converge in New York and then all split up. It just seemed to me to be resonant. The title has a very beautiful kind of sound to it. And the idea of authority itself: who's compelling them to speak at all? The ambiguity of, "Do they have a choice?"

GW: In early interviews, you said you expected the audience to bring a certain degree of reason and order to the theatre experience. Would you say a few things about what ideally you would like to happen to the audience during one of your plays?

CMcP: I think instinctively I just want to entertain them. Also communicate with them. And give them the opportunity (though I don't mean this in any vocational sense) to communicate with each other as an audience, too. They tend to react as a group. When they're watching something, people try to figure out what's happening, especially if it's not the three-act play, where a gun goes off in the first act and in the third they know what they are going to get. Like Sean O'Casey always said, the sign of a good play is that it divides critics and audiences. The more I go on with my work, there are more people who say, "I don't get him." And there is a kind of resentment among critics that other people are enjoying it. And I think that's because I'm respecting the audience to make of it what they will. That's our human instinct, and that's how good ad campaigns work. They give you things which you put together yourself. That means you will remember it because you spent more time on it. As a playwright or theatre director, I am becoming more confident and still accessible. I don't think I'm going to make a strange mathematical conundrum the hinge of the play, in a Tom Stoppard kind of way. It's really just a stage on which ordinary human emotions are expressed very simply.

GW: Is the film audience essentially the same as that for theatre? Or do you think of them differently?

CMcP: Well, I think you have to sell a film. A film like *Saltwater* is not going to compete with *Pearl Harbour*. It just doesn't have the resources. If you sell it right and are honest about what it is, it will find its audience. There are audiences who wouldn't go near *Pearl Harbour* or *Jurassic Park*. They see those as summer movies and look for what else is on. As a filmmaker, I am into what else is on. (He laughs.) I'm not saying that at this point I have anything revolutionary to offer, just simple stories about simple people. Maybe my characters are a bit mad, but they are not trying to drill a hole in the universe with an asteroid, like in *Armageddon*. And they never will.

GW: You've said that it is easy for you to move from theatre to film because your own work, even in plays, is essentially visual.

CMcP: What I loved about the filmmaking process was post-production, where I discovered that a person's face was really as interesting as what they were saying. Sometimes we would just cut the lines, which I don't think made the actors too happy (he laughs), but visually human beings are just interested in other human beings. John Ford was in the middle of some desert shooting a western, and the first assistant director says to him, "Well, what do you want to start with,

John? What is the first shot?" And Ford says, "Well, we're going to shoot the most interesting thing on the planet. I'm going to shoot the human face." *Saltwater* was low budget. And because we didn't have a lot of time, the most interesting thing I had was the actors. And I hope I wasn't stupid enough to ignore that fact. When I got the chance to make *Endgame* as a film, I couldn't change a thing because of the Beckett estate. That actually made post-production easier because I had no choice.

GW: In your recent work, one character says history is dead. Another says language is dead. And there does seem to be an increasing tension in your work between the traditional world of morality and the post-modern world of licence and play. Are you aware of such tensions?

CMcP: I suppose I do instinctively play with that tension. There are all the people who are given the map to life, which is: go to school, leave school, work, get married, have children, pay a mortgage, go on holiday, your parents die, then you die, and then your kids die, like Joe in *Port Authority*, who says, "I came from a time when you didn't need to be asking questions like you do now." *Port Authority* has that tension between negotiability being easy for one generation and for another generation not so. I give them the map, and they don't see it. They see their parents divorced or an older brother's drug addiction. It's a little bit more wide open for them. But I think my characters always tend to find an innate sense of what's right and wrong, or at least worry about it and usually come back to traditional moral law, which is basically utilitarian: If I don't treat other people well, I may not get treated well myself. The characters come back to the fear of not being loved. But my plays always have characters who are shown an opportunity to break out. The whole play is about whether they do or don't. In my plays they usually don't, or they do for a little while and they come back. And nobody can answer that for them; everybody learns different ways of dealing with it.

GW: The early works seem a celebration of voices and stories; the middle works include ethical dilemmas involving others. But in *Port Authority*, the images and potential relationships are just there, and the audience is asked to respond, to think about it.

CMcP: Even in *Dublin Carol* I wasn't allowing the main character, John, to have the freedom of the monologue, in which the character can tell how he or she perceives things. The other characters get tired of it and ask him to be accountable. And yet I think it still reaches the same kind of conclusion as the other plays. That is, if you are going to be crippled by fear, if that is what drives you into a shell and you can't cope, you are really powerless. I don't know if that is an optimistic or a pessimistic play. But what I was doing was taking the type of character that I normally write about — who would see himself as a kind of hero, who says, "This is what I do. I did it all the way I fucking wanted to. Fuck you" — and put him back in a world where two people of a different generation question him with "Why? What are you afraid of? Why are you so afraid?" And there really is no answer. In *Dublin Carol*, his daughter says, "I think about you." And he says, "Why? Why do you think about me?" And she says, "Well, because I love you." And actually to write that kind of line with no irony in a play just blows the fucking thing apart. And you go, "Fuck, where do we go from here?" And he goes, "Well, I think about you, too." (He laughs.) You are again presenting someone with a choice.

GW: You have said that you like Billy Roche's work because he has the courage to write about love without irony.

CMcP: Yeah. The world is full of people with broken hearts. It's the saying of it to each other, you know: "You broke my heart." I remember I used to read plays by someone like Chekhov, and people are just bursting into tears all over the place, saying, "Why don't you love me?" And I thought it was terrible. And then you see a good production with good actors doing it and it rips your heart out. And then it can become boring, which is the other end of the spectrum, can become a maudlin kind of play. Which just brings me back to the point that really you have to be collaborative because a good actor will say with such conviction the things that you never think you'll get away with, that he will carry it.

GW: Clearly you were focused on such concerns as a student of psychology, English and philosophy at UCD [University College Dublin]. But were you interested in these ethical issues when you were a child? Did you read a lot?

CMcP: There were always a lot of books in the house. And I was never constrained about what I could or could not read. I had two sisters, one older and one younger. And I think our parents were just glad if we were reading anything. I learned everything about sex and grown-up stuff through books at a very young age. I was reading books like *Clockwork Orange* when I was nine or ten. You didn't get some of it. But when you had read three books in a row that had penetration, you began to realise that the man sticks his penis into the woman. (He laughs.) And eventually you have to ask somebody.

GW: So who did you ask, and how did it work out?

CMcP: You asked people in school because there were kids in school who knew. "Yeah, you don't know that?" And you are only nine. "You don't know that yet? That's how you have babies." And you wonder what that's got to do with having babies. But it's amazing that you can read that stuff as a kid and if you don't get it, just skip it. I always remember a line from a Stephen King novel I read when I was young. This couple start to have sex, and you find that quite boring because all you want is the horror, and I thought, "Oh, here they go." And I read, "Her panties were gone in a whisper." That line has always stuck with me. I think it was the onomatopoeia of the sound of her panties being taken off, or the whisper, "Can I take off your panties?" But that is the only sexual thing that has stayed with me from my childhood. Or, in *A Clockwork Orange*, he talks about him standing there with a "panhandle", which, you know, is an erection. I learned a lot, thinking it was OK to have erections.

GW: It sounds like the Catholic family gave you room to play.

CMcP: Yeah. My father didn't go to mass. My mother did. With all the children's stuff going on, there was really no pressure like that, religiously.

GW: In some of your recent plays, you seem to me to be coming back to religious imagery, in *Port Authority* but even before that in *Dublin Carol*.

CMcP: Well, yeah, for one thing it is very beautiful, aesthetically. Catholicism is based so much around imagery. What Protestants would call idolatry.

GW: Some Protestants.

CMcP: Well, yeah, the people who protest against Catholicism. Those images when you are a young kid do stay with you. Jesus' heart is on fire, he's nailed to this cross, a crown of thorns, his mother grieving at the foot of his cross. It's powerful stuff. You are saying this to kids who are five and six. You are also saying there's a place called hell and there's a very strong possibility you are going to go there, you five-year-old fucker. It's got to affect some kids more than others. And I think the guilt and fear that you are essentially a bad person who needs to be redeemed stays with some kids. The alcohol withdrawal that Irish people feel when they drink every day has a natural, physiological effect. But that is also bound up with the bad weather and the Catholic belief that you are a bad person letting everybody down anyway.

And that's why I think there is a very strong storytelling and playwriting tradition for such a small country. The people can exorcise their fears through these "what-if" scenarios. Not to say that everybody's writing autobiographically. But they are taking elements of their own lives and saying, "What if I were to leave my family and go for that love of my life, that job I always wanted, or rob a bank, or just drop out?" It spurs the imagination into working out what the possible consequences of such actions might be without having to do that. Now I think this culture of fear is disappearing. When I was 16, there was nowhere to go in Dublin. I remember I had a girlfriend, and it was Valentine's Day, a Sunday, and there was nothing to do. But my younger sister is seven years younger than me, and she and her friends are so confident. They feel this is their city; they are so happy and carefree. They were not brought up under a school system which allowed religious bashing. But getting back to the point about Catholicism, there is something very beautiful about it. The idea of forgiveness and redemption. I guess it is kind of the culture of the hangover, you know.

GW: Do you consider yourself a Catholic writer?

CMcP: I see myself as someone who was educated as a Catholic, not a Catholic writer. I think I write a detailed response to singular experiences.

GW: Other than that you grew up in North Dublin and continue to live in Ireland, what makes your writing Irish?

CMcP: It is the whole notion of Catholicism and the idea of the spiritual world somehow being more real than the material world. Irish people are more concerned about the inner life . . . and the inner response. A monologue gets into what people really think, which is entertaining and exciting because people don't normally tell us what they really think. It is also what they think makes sense. Or what they think sounds rational. But they don't actually express the more primal thing, which is the voice that is in there.

GW: How would you explain this to a post-modernist, who believes there is no such thing as the self or an inner life?

CMcP: Even when nothing particularly bad is happening, some people can feel a kind of injustice, a kind of primal anger. That's coming from somewhere. Deep in them they have an idea of how things should be and how they should occur. And they become upset when they see things, which may not necessarily have a huge impact on them personally, which give them a sense of right and wrong. I think it is that little anger that becomes embodied in me as a kind of mischievousness. In my stuff I just want to keep pushing it, I want to blow everything apart. Just get everybody to look at each other.

GW: You turn anger into experimentation.

CMcP: Sure. It comes down to the strange fault line between being mischievous and being responsible. It's not just mischievousness for its own sake. It's not just "Look at me. I'm angry." It's "Look at this. Isn't it funny? Are we laughing because it's wrong to do these things, because it's deviant? Or because we want to be deviant?" It's really those questions I am interested in rather than just the cocky and the snooty.

GW: I'm thinking of the last images of *Port Authority*, Dermot with his head in the lap of his wife and Joe with his arms folded, holding a rosary. Those are images of compassion, but they aren't just moving because they are religious or Catholic. You've used them to recover something very essential.

CMcP: I think my plays get produced in so many different countries because what I'm writing about is not a specific agenda at a specific time. There is a universality of concern, which is the basic fear of being alone. How long do my parents have to live? How am I going to provide for such-and-such a person who I know is sick? Who's going to look after me when I'm sick? Those are the most important things. Fear and love are universal. To me they are what's worth writing about. People have a huge thirst just for recognition: "Oh, you are afraid, too." I think Beckett took that to an extreme and made it very formal: "We're alone. Deal with it. Laugh at it. Shout at it." But I think I'm a bit gentler. "Yeah, you are alone. I don't know how we are going to deal with it." Maybe there's nothing to figure out. Maybe it is enough for someone to say, "It breaks my heart that you've been having a problem. I know you don't want to talk about it. But just so you know, I'm here if you want to give me a shout or whatever." Those things are really much more important than your standing in your academic department or your bank or where you are being published. So much more important is the tiniest gesture; someone putting their hand on your arm is huge and can mean more to you than winning money or anything like that. I think those are the things that travel in my plays, the details, a smell or someone describing how their feet felt on the ground.

GW: *Saltwater* ends with such small gestures, Ray saying you know me, meaning he is not going to change, or the boy at the ocean feeling all these new adult realities.

CMcP: I'll tell you a funny thing that happened that day. We had a new camera operator in the last week of filming. Because he hadn't had time to read the script, he asked me, "What is this shot? What are you trying to do?" And I said, "Well, it's the last shot of the film, and he comes to this school and they are just going to meet in the frame." Someone reported to me that this camera operator said during the shooting, "So that's the last shot of the film?" And the guy says, "Yeah." And he goes, "Should they not be smiling?" (He laughs.) And it is a legitimate question: Why aren't they smiling?

GW: What would you tell him?

CMcP: Just read the script. But it is a quite wide-open ending. The financers were like "I don't get it. What's the hidden meaning?" And there was no hidden meaning. He's going to see this girl, take responsibility, which means everything. At one point they were saying, "Shouldn't he have a voiceover to explain . . . ?" But I didn't want anything which would keep it bound to its theatrical beginnings. So there's no voiceovers or monologues in the film.

GW: A recent review of *Saltwater* says the title refers to nothing in the movie, but the film actually opens and closes with images of the beach, the place where the land meets the ocean.

CMcP: At the end of the film, Joe is with his brother, who is leaving. He cries and then he gets on his bike and goes to see this girl. It's all played out against the background of an environment we can't live in, which is the sea. So it's also about reaching a limit. There is nowhere else to go; he has to come back and live or die. It's about tears and taking responsibility.

GW: We haven't talked much about *The Weir*, the play which brought you so much attention and success. How do you feel about it now?

CMcP: I don't know. I don't think anything about it, you know? (He laughs.)

GW: I imagined you'd say, "Well, I still like the play. I think it is really good. But then I started to have to deal with all this stuff."

CMcP: Yeah. Well, again, the audience made that play what it is. I mean I wrote it when I was 24. I didn't sit down to write a play that was going to be a big commercial success. I remember saying at the time, "The play is a bunch of people sitting together in a pub telling each other ghost stories." It didn't sound like a good idea. It sounded like a pretty bad idea. But I thought it could really work. It was only supposed to run for three or so weeks in a 60-seat capacity theatre. It just took on a life of its own. It's about fundamental fear. And the powerful need people have for community, between two people, or three people, or a hundred and three people.

GW: All these men seem to be interested in attracting this woman, in one way or another, not necessarily in a predatory way. But when she tells her story, then empathy and compassion have an opportunity.

CMcP: Yeah. And they do it in different ways. Yeah, you are right. There isn't anything else I can say.

GW: And I think people get it.

CMcP: It's very simple. It is the impact, really, of what she says. I would hate to think that people would see that play as a woman's inability to tell a story and then suddenly her ability to tell the story. It is about what happens when she tells the story and what it means to everybody. It can be quite disappointing when people say it is just a bunch of Irish people telling stories. I know that there is an awful lot of bad theatre, bad movies, bad books — a lot of mediocre, boring stuff out there. But essentially I would like to think that I am a kind of bright person, that my whole goal isn't just to place myself among a bunch of [Irish] writers. My ambition, if I have ambition, is to do something more personally provocative.

GW: When I saw *The Weir* with a number of people who were studying theatre on an NEH grant at Columbia University, we thought it was by far the best play out that summer. And yet when the reviews came out, they were lukewarm, indicating a kind of reluctance among New York reviewers to like yet another Irish playwright. How aware are you of the differences in responses, especially by critics, in Ireland, England, and the US, or any place else, for that matter?

CMcP: I'm as sensitive as anybody. I think that if anybody gives *The Weir* a bad review, I honestly think they're a bad critic. It's just that simple.

GW: The well-made play, which makes people comfortable, can actually be very limiting by pretending to say something artificially conclusive. Your work is actually closer to real life because it presents the ambiguity in which the audience has to judge the speaker, to say, "Now he's lying."

CMcP: If you want to write a tragedy, there's only a right way and a wrong way. I don't know if my writing is tragedy or comedy . . . or what it is. Probably closer to comedy, though there are still a lot of sad things. I'm very precise about my work, about how I do it. But at its core it is a mess, like life is, rather than about a neat idea. That's what I like about *Lime Tree Bower* and *Port Authority*, where the characters don't refer to each other, or even know each other, but each one seems to sort of reflect the other one somehow, to enlighten the other, to make it resonate differently. It's the gap between the speakers, where all this is going on, and I have no idea of what that is. It's the stuff that we don't say that really intrigues me. I am actually playing with the theatre. I am in the very lucky position of managing to stretch the boundaries of what the audience will tolerate in the theatre.

GW: What do you say to people who criticise how women are portrayed in your plays and films?

CMcP: If you are a younger writer, it feels like critics are giving you points in an exam. OK, he can write a story: 50 per cent. But can he write dialogue? Well, OK: 60 per cent. But can he write for women? And the implication of that kind of reviewing is that actresses, technicians, and women who go see my work are inherently stupid because they don't know they are getting a rough time or helping to prolong my sexist agenda against themselves. It is insulting to the women who work with me.

GW: The American playwright Horton Foote says all of his plays are about why some people can find the courage to face their fears and others can't. And you say fear is a central to your plays as well.

CMcP: Yeah, I think plays like *Port Authority*, *The Weir*, and *Dublin Carol* are about people not having the courage to break the mould or face the moral responsibility to do what they think is correct. If you are in a loveless marriage, do you have a responsibility to yourself, to your wife, to end it? Or do you have a responsibility to your children, to your wife or husband, to stay for the sake of stability? Do you sacrifice your own happiness for other people's? And what principles are you prepared to sacrifice? Those are moral decisions. And I think very many people sacrifice their own happiness — just to fit in. They settle for second best, or third best.

Now, at the other end of the scale, you have those people who don't settle for second best, and maybe are regarded as very selfish people. But perhaps their honesty in the long run is liberating to people by their example. And then there are the fucking bastards who are so selfish they are not a good example for anybody. And really it just goes back to that basic thing, like Aristotle, that really the secret to happiness is moderation. I know it is a boring answer. But it's a mixture of being able to be a bit crazy when you need to be and also standing your ground when you need to, to protect those around you and yourself. I think people make moral decisions everyday, not thinking about them as moral decisions. But they are. It's how you define yourself, through your actions — all the time.

GW: In your master's thesis, you defend utilitarianism. Have you changed your position?

CMcP: No. I think people basically are hedonists. But having said that, I have a very broad view of what gives people pleasure, extremely broad, to encompass everything.

GW: As a writer, then, you dramatise people making choices about their kinds of pleasure. Yours is neither a liberationist nor a moralistic theatre.

CMcP: Yeah. I really don't think I have an agenda or a message. All I can say is my work is a battle against loneliness. It's an acknowledgement that we all have a fundamental loneliness even though you may not be alone. But all that loneliness can be eased by admitting and sharing that fact. Having said that, it does not necessarily mean that my work is bleak. I don't think it is. I think it is quite optimistic because its intention is to make contact, to make connection. It's really that simple.

GW: Do you think it was your training in ethics and philosophy that caused you to ask such questions?

CMcP: Studying philosophy taught me that I don't really know very much, but neither does anybody else. We're all just guessing. And it's OK to say stupid things, to have a stab, as long as we are tolerant of people who are also having a stab. You can see the attraction of fanaticism because it's so clear when most people are muddy people. It's like your asking if I believe in socialism. As a principle, I would love to see it happen. But I don't know if it is compatible with human nature to ask people to share everything. People get fearful and begin to hoard stuff. I think we can solve the problem of poverty; it is well within our grasp. But we don't have the leadership, and that's because of our doubts. That's why someone like George W. Bush scares me. It's like Hitler was asked when he was standing in his library, "Have you read all these books?" And he said, "I don't need to read. I've already made up my mind." I'm afraid of people who are so sure of everything. I think it is OK to say stupid things, just to see what people will do. I think you have to have a certain amount of mischief, be able to say, "I think you are a twit", just to see what will happen. But to believe them is another thing.

GW: It's like we used to say about Nixon. "I hope he is just being a politician. My God, what if he actually believes what he is saying?"

CMcP: Did you see that film *The Contender*? That was one of the best films I've seen about the Presidency. He was portrayed as a pragmatist, who has to fuck people. You don't become President of the United States unless you are willing to fuck people. You don't become Prime Minister of a country by not ruining people's careers. It just has to be done. The film portrayed the President in that kind of way, which I thought was OK. Ironically, Bush is too idealistic, and he thinks he's doing what is right. It's so funny. But then there was Carter, who was a very democratic President but just wasn't enough of a bastard.

GW: You seem terribly busy. But when you have time to go to plays or movies, who do you pay attention to?

CMcP: Billy Roche, Harold Pinter, Beckett, Tom Murphy, Brian Friel. I like some younger British writers at the moment. Joe Penhall, especially his new play, called *Blue/Orange*, which is going to Broadway, I think. He's fantastic. A bit of everything here and there. Among American playwrights I like David Mamet's work, Lanford Wilson, David Ives.

GW: Any filmmakers that you are especially drawn to?

CMcP: I love Woody Allen's films. He makes disparate stuff. I like *Crimes and Misdemeanours*, which is such a powerful film about guilt. It's just incredible. And then *Manhattan* is such a powerful film about love, so beautiful. Again he plays a smartass who is always talking, making jokes, and when he tries to break up with the character played by Mariel Hemingway, and she just starts crying and can't understand why he is breaking up . . . it's just such a sweet moment. And you think, yeah, this is what break-ups are like, and you realise what he's doing. It's such a simple idea. And gradually this close-up on her while he's telling her. He says, "You've got your whole life ahead of you. I'm old." "But," she says, "I love you." It's that simple. "I don't understand why you are saying this to me." It's really heartbreaking. And yet the wisecracks are flying all over the place. Like when he's standing at that party and this woman says, "I managed to have an orgasm finally, but my doctor said it's the wrong kind." And he says, "Even my worst ones have been pretty much right on the money." And I like it in *Annie Hall* when this guy is on the phone and says, "Yeah. Yeah. Yeah. I'm calling long distance. Tell him I forgot my mantra." (He laughs.)

GW: What are you working on now?

CMcP: I'm going to direct a film, which Neil Jordan is producing, a comedy about actors. It's just called *The Actors*. And I did research on and wrote a screenplay for a film which is set in Alabama and Georgia. But I don't know what I'm going to do with that yet.

GW: Were you doing that yourself?

CMcP: I was working with Paddy [Breathnach]. Basically it's about a black woman who works in a deputy sheriff's office, in a small Southern town which is about to have a bicentennial. About a week before the celebration, she stops someone who's speeding, which leads to a car chase. He crashes, and she arrests him. And when they run his prints, they find out he's listed as dead. He's in a witness protection pro-

gramme, but he's just committed a murder. The FBI are trying to get him out. And there are people who want him killed.
The main protagonist is studying for a sergeant's exam in this
sleepy town. We haven't really shown it to anybody because
Paddy's gone off to make another film. But we've been talking
about it again, looking at it again.

GW: It seems strange that you would move from a play like
Port Authority, which is set so clearly in Dublin, to the American South.

CMcP: Well, we went over and I interviewed sheriffs and
federal agents down in that area, spoke to them about how
they work.

GW: How was that?

CMcP: It was an experience. (He laughs.) It was fun, but a bit
scary. Claustrophobic. That very strong Baptist thing. Dry
counties . . . not like New York. We went down as far as
New Orleans. That seemed so debauched in comparison with
some places that were so clean and clean-living. In the middle
of nowhere, at an exit just outside the county line, would be
this huge strip bar, with all these pick-up trucks around it. I
thought it sort of weird.

GW: Was that story an idea that you had, or you and Paddy
shared?

CMcP: When we made *I Went Down*, we didn't want to
make a film that was specifically Irish. It was a film which
played with genre, the buddy movie, with elements of film
noir, and put together to see if it works here [Ireland]. And
then we thought, "Well, let's do the rainy, deep South, *Angel*

Heart, In the Heat of the Night, Midnight in the Garden of Good and Evil, Badlands type movie."

GW: It is interesting that in film you accept the burden of genre whereas in theatre you are so interested in breaking rules, doing things against the grain, and finding new freedom.

CMcP: It's a bit strange. The cinema audiences respond to marketability. It's that old saying that if you can say in one sentence what it's about, people are more likely to go to it. But if it takes a half hour to explain what this film's about, people will say, "I don't have time." I don't know why that is.

GW: I hope you get that film made.

CMcP: Well, we'll see, you know. It is a strange world, the film world.

GW: How did the film with Neil Jordan come to be?

CMcP: He had an idea, and he rang me to see if I would write it as a screenplay, for him to direct. It's a comedy. And when he saw *Saltwater*, he said, "You should direct it."

GW: Where will it be shot?

CMcP: Dublin. I go into pre-production in January. So shooting should begin in March of 2002.

GW: So what's in your immediate future?

CMcP: We are doing Eugene O'Brien's play [*Eden*], which we did it in the Abbey's smaller space, The Peacock. Now we're in The Abbey. I will direct that again. So, Eugene's play before

Christmas, then *The Actors* film, which will commit me, probably, until September 2002.

GW: Are there plans for more of your plays to be produced in the United States?

CMcP: Yes. We haven't done *Dublin Carol* or *Port Authority* there because I haven't had time to oversee the productions. But I will. The Manhattan Theatre Club want to do the American premiere of *Port Authority*. They want it to open in March, but I won't be able to be around, and if it is a production with new actors, I want to be there.

GW: Are you becoming more sensitive to the need to maintain control over the productions?

CMcP: The first time, yes. It prolongs the life of the play because if it is a good production, if it works, then people will be interested in seeing other productions of it. And there is an opportunity to do *Dublin Carol* on Broadway and also Steppenwolf wanted to do it in Chicago. But basically I'll set some time aside in a few months or a year, whatever, when I can find time to spend some time in the States, with those two plays

Bibliography

Articles, Books and Plays by Conor McPherson

McPherson, Conor (1993), "Logical Constraint and Practical Reasoning: On Attempted Refutations of Utilitarianism", unpublished Master's thesis, Dublin: University College.

McPherson, Conor (1996), *This Lime Tree Bower: Three Plays* [includes *This Lime Tree Bower*, *Rum and Vodka*, *The Good Thief*] London and Dublin: Nick Hern/New Island.

McPherson, Conor (et al.) (1997a), *I Went Down: the Shooting Script*, London: Nick Hern.

McPherson, Conor (1997b), *St Nicholas and The Weir: Two Plays*, Dublin: New Island Books; Nick Hern Books.

McPherson, Conor (1998a), *The Weir*, London: Nick Hern.

McPherson, Conor (1998b), "If you're a young Irish playwright, come to London. If you can put up with being defined by your nationality, the opportunities are huge", *New Statesman*, 127 (20 February), 40–41.

McPherson, Conor (1999a), "24 hours with Meryl Streep", *Harper's Bazaar* (January), 124–27.

McPherson, Conor (1999b), "Late Night and Proclamations", *American Theatre*, 16 (April), 45–46.

McPherson, Conor (1999c), *McPherson: Four Plays* [includes *This Lime Tree Bower, St Nicholas, Rum and Vodka, The Good Thief*] London: Nick Hern.

McPherson, Conor (1999d), *Salzwasser*, Berlin: Friedrich Berlin.

McPherson, Conor (1999e), *The Weir and Other Plays* [includes *The Weir, St Nicholas, This Lime Tree Bower, The Good Thief, Rum and Vodka*] New York: Theatre Communications Group.

McPherson, Conor (1999f), *The Weir*, New York: Dramatists Play Service.

McPherson, Conor (1999g), "Old Ireland bad, New Ireland good", *Irish Times* (30 December), www.ireland.com.

McPherson, Conor (2000a), "We are masters of illusion", *Irish Times* (May 23), 12.

McPherson, Conor (2000b), *Dublin Carol*, London: Nick Hern.

McPherson, Conor (2000c), *Dublin Carol: A Play*, New York: Theatre Communications Group.

McPherson, Conor (2001a), "Chapter Two", *Yeats is Dead*, ed. Joseph O'Connor. London: Random House.

McPherson, Conor (2001b), *Come On Over*, Unpublished manuscript used by permission of author.

McPherson, Conor (2001c), *Port Authority*, London: Nick Hern.

McPherson, Conor (2001d), *Saltwater: The Shooting Script*, London: Nick Hern.

McPherson, Conor (2001e), "Original sin", *The Guardian* (7 February), www.guardian.co.uk.

McPherson, Conor (2001f), "Standing in the bold boys' corner — aged 3", *Education & Living online with The Irish Times*, www.ireland.com/education/el/finalbell/2001/1016/story1.htm.

McPherson, Conor (2001g), "Another year, another struggle", *Education & Living online with The Irish Times*, www.ireland.com/education/el/finalbell/2001/1016/story2.htm.

McPherson, Conor (2001h), "Billy Roche", in Lilian Chambers, Ger FitzGibbon, Eamonn Jordan, Dan Farrelly and Cathy Leeney (eds.), *Theatre Talk: Voices of Irish Theatre Practitioners*, Dublin: Carysfort Press, 409–23.

Interviews with Conor McPherson

Adams, Tim (2001), "So there's these three Irishmen . . .", *The Observer* (4 February), www.observer.co.uk.

Allen, Carol (2001), "Camera happy", *The Times* (4 January), www.newsint-archive.co.uk.

Carty, Ciaran (2000a), "Saltwater in His Eyes", *Sunday Tribune* (24 September), 2.

Clarke, Donald (2003), "Fighting Demons", *The Irish Times*, Weekend Review (10 May), 7.

"Conor McPherson; Interview" (2001), *The Times* (17 February), www.newsint-archive.co.uk.

Duane, Paul (1997), "I Wrote Down", *Film Ireland* (October/November), 14–15.

Greenstreet, Rosanna (2001), "The questionnaire", *The Guardian Weekend* (17 March), www.guardian.co.uk.

Heaney, Mick (1999), "A Touch of Class", *London Sunday Times* (30 May), 21.

Hourihane, Ann Marie (1998), "The Play's the Thing", *The Sunday Tribune Magazine* (15 March), 6–7.

Keogh, Carol, "Conor McPherson Interview", www.theblackrag.com/vol7/out.htm.

McKenzie, Will (2001a), "Conor McPherson Interview", *6degrees: The Film Connection* (January), www.6degrees.co.uk /en/2/200101ftconor.html.

"McPherson on Beckett", *Beckett on Film (Endgame)*, www.channel4.com.

O'Connell, Jennifer (2000), "Class Acts", *Sunday Business Post* (15 October), 37–38.

"The Pint of No Return" (2002), *Village Voice*, vol. 47, no. 42 (11 October), 60.

Renner, Pamela (1998), "Haunts of the Very Irish", *American Theatre*, vol. 15, no. 6 (July–August), 20–21, 62–63.

Soloski, Alexis (2002), "Drinking in America", *Time Out New York* (10–17 October), www.timeoutny.com.

Vincent, Sally (2002), "Funny, peculiar", *The Guardian* (13 July), www.guardian.co.uk.

White, Victoria (1998), "Telling stories in the dark", *Irish Times* (2 July), www.ireland.com.

Whitehead, Sam (1999), "*Weir* science", *Time Out New York* (25 March – 1 April), www.timeoutny.com.

Wolf, Matt (1998a), "A Darling of the Critics Who Doesn't Flatter Them", *New York Times* (15 March), AR8.

Articles and Essays on McPherson's Work in Books and Journals

The Actors, The Press Release, Film Four, February 2003.

Barry, Kevin (1997), "Conor Cannes do", *Irish Times* (17 May), www.ireland.com.

Billington, Michael (2000), "A Study in despair", *The Guardian* (22 January), www.guardian.co.uk.

Billington, Michael (2001), "Conor McPherson's Cocaine and Cardigans", *The Guardian* (24 February), www.guardian.co. uk.

Bradshaw, Peter (2001), "Robbery with chips", *The Guardian* (5 January), www.guardian.co.uk.

Brantley, Ben (1998), "A Most Dramatic Drama Critic", *New York Times* (18 March), www.nytimes.com.

Brantley, Ben (1999a), "Dark Yarns Casting Light", *New York Times* (2 April), B1, 26.

Brantley, Ben (1999b), "A Wealth Of Ambiguity, An Economy Of Words", *New York Times* (20 May), www.nytimes.com.

Brantley, Ben (2001), "A Hired Thug Who Lacks the Typical Heart of Gold", *New York Times* (13 March), B1, 5.

Brantley, Ben (2003), "When Talk Is the Cure for the Morning After", *New York Times* (21 February), www.nytimes. com.

Brustein, Robert (1999), "Robert Brustein on Theatre — Spring Roundup", *New Republic* (7 June), 32–34.

Cagle, Jess (1999), "Shock Treatment: Two London Imports Give Audiences a Jolt", *Entertainment Weekly* (9 April), 66.

Canby, Vincent (1999), "Only On the Stage Does 'Iceman' Truly Come Alive", *New York Times* (18 April), AR8.

Carty, Ciaran (2000b), "*Borstal Boy* and *Saltwater* worth their weight as movies", *Sunday Tribune* (23 July), 7.

Clapp, Susannah (2001), "Is Conor McPherson simply too good for the stage?", *The Observer* (25 February), www.observer. co.uk.

Christopher, James (1998), "The problem with Irish road movies is that you arrive too soon", *The Observer* (January 25), www.observer.co.uk.

Cote, David (2002), "*Rum and Vodka*", *Time Out New York* (17–24 October), www.timeoutny.com.

Cox, Brian (1999), "The Loneliness, Elation and Doubts of the Monologuist", *New York Times* (16 May), www.nytimes.com.

Cummings, Scott. T. (2000), "Homo Fabulator: The Narrative Imperative in Conor McPherson's Plays", in Eamonn Jordan (ed.), *Theatre Stuff: Critical Essays on Contemporary Irish Theatre*, Dublin: Carysfort Press, 303–12.

Day-Lewis, Tamasin (1999), "Ghost of a Chance", *Vogue* (April), 220.

Dromgoole, Dominic (2002), "Conor MacPherson [sic]", *The Full Room, An A–Z of Contemporary Playwriting*, London: Methuen, 186–89.

"'Dublin Carol': Rich, Rueful Meditation" (2003), *New York Times* (20 February), www.nytimes.com.

Dwyer, Michael (2000), "Looking up after 'I Went Down'", *Irish Times* (23 September), www.ireland.com.

Elley, Derek (1997), "I Went Down", *Variety* (13 October), 98.

Feingold, Michael (1999), "The Weir", *Village Voice* 44 (13 April), 159.

Franks, Alan (1999), "Ireland's Sober Voice", *The Times* (11 December), Features, 45.

French, Philip (2001), "Saltwater", *The Observer* (7 January), www.guardian.co.uk.

Fricker, Karen (1998), "Eire cheers 'Weir' Hometown Boy McPherson's Play Bows in Dublin", *Variety* (20–26 July), 49.

Fricker, Karen (2001), "Three Short Plays", *The Guardian* (11 October), www.guardian.co.uk.

Friedlander, Mira (1998), "The Weir", *Variety* 370 (4–10 May), 94.

Gamerman, Amy (1999a), "Theatre: Barroom Spellbinders", *Wall Street Journal* (7 April), A20.

Gamerman, Amy (1999b), "Theatre: Pakistan Meets West", *Wall Street Journal* (26 May), A20.

Gamerman, Amy (2001), "Theatre: Love Triangulation", *Wall Street Journal* (21 March), A20.

Gardner, Lyn (2001), "Rum and Vodka/The Good Thief", *The Guardian* (3 May), www.guardian.co.uk.

Glacken, Brendan (2001), "Lads, we are totally useless", *Irish Times* (2 March), www.ireland.com.

Gussow, Mel (1999), "From Dublin to Broadway, Spinning Tales of Irish Wool", *New York Times* (1 April), B1, 3.

Hitchcock, Laura (2001), "Pub Pop", *Back Stage West* 8 (25 January), 16.

Holland, Jonathan (2000), "10 European directors to watch", *Variety*, 377 (7–13 February), 44–46.

Hornby, Richard (1999), "The Weir", *Hudson Review*, 52 (Autumn), 465.

Isherwood, Charles (1999), "The Weir", *Variety*, 374 (5–11 April), 154.

Jenson, Hal (1997), "Old cod with relish", *Times Literary Supplement* (18 July), 20.

Jensen, Hal (1997), "St Nicholas", *Times Literary Supplement* (7 March), 19.

Jones, Chris (1998), "St Nicholas", *Variety*, 370 (23–29 March), 98–99.

Kanfer, Stefan (1999), "Taxing Imports", *New Leader* (19 April), 21–22.

Kellaway, Kate (1996), "Ian Rickson at the Royal Court", *New Statesman*, 11 (6 February), 40.

Kellaway, Kate (2000), "Irish Pinter", *New Statesman*, 13 (7 February), 44–45.

Kelly, Richard (2001), "Saltwater", *Sight and Sound* (January), 58.

Kemp, Philip (1998), "I Went Down", *Sight and Sound* (February), 44–45.

Kilroy, Ian (2000), "Learning to be happy", *Irish Times*, (30 August), 5.

King, Robert L. (2000a), "Simple and Panoramic", *North American Review* (May–August), 71.

King, Robert L. (2000b), "The Irish and Others", *North American Review* (November), 43.

Kroll, Jack (1999), "When Irish Guys Are Beguiling: Finding poetry in a pub", *Newsweek* (12 April), 77.

Lahr, John (1999), "The Bayjaysus Factor", *New Yorker* (12 April), 101–2.

Linehan, Hugh (2000), "Saltwater", *Film West*, 42 (Winter), 58.

Lyons, Donald (1998), "Theatre: From Apocalypse to Comic Relief", *Wall Street Journal* (2 April), A20.

MacNab, Geoffrey (2001), "Saltwater", *Sight and Sound*, 11 (October), 65.

Margolies, Dany (2002), "Stage Spot", *Back Stage West* 9 (August 29), 13.

Maslin, Janet (1998), "Cavorting in Irish Gangland", *New York Times* (24 June), www.nytimes.com.

McCarthy, Gerry (2000a), "Not so likely lad", *Sunday Times* (16 July), 9.

McCarthy, Gerry (2000b), "Saltwater", *Film Ireland* 77 (August/September), 15–17.

McKenzie, Will (2001b), "Saltwater", *6degrees: The Film Connection* (January), www.6degrees.co.uk /en/2/200101frsaltwater1.html.

McLoone, Martin (1999), "Reimagining the Nation: Theme and Issues in Irish Cinema", *Cineaste*, vol. 24, nos. 2–3 (March), 28–34.

McNulty, Charles (1999), "This Lime Tree Bower", *Variety* (May 24), 78.

Morgenstern, Joe (1998), "Film: Cosmic Crashes; Comic Cons", *Wall Street Journal* (1 July), A16.

Morley, Sheridan (1997), "A Lost World", *Spectator*, 278 (8 March), 43–44.

Morley, Sheridan (1998), "Truth Will Out", *Spectator*, 280 (7 March), 44.

Morley, Sheridan (2001), "West End Shame", *Spectator*, 286 (10 March), 50.

Nightingale, Benedict (1997a), "Vitriol personified", *The Times* (25 February), www.newsint-archive.co.uk.

Nightingale, Benedict (1997b), "Spooks' night at the pub", *The Times* (11 July), www.newsint-achive.co.uk.

Nightingale, Benedict (1998a), "Another round in the Irish bar", *The Times* (25 February), www.newsint-archive.co.uk.

Nightingale, Benedict (1998b), "Fear, Apathy, Regret: A Happy Combination", *New York Times* (15 March), AR8, 18.

Nightingale, Benedict (2000a), "Trace of hope amid drink and contempt", *The Times* (21 January), www.newsint-archive.co.uk.

Nightingale, Benedict (2000b), "The big play: Dublin Carol", *The Times* (5 February), www.newsint-archive.co.uk.

Nightingale, Benedict (2000c), "A Mortician's Confessions in Shades of Boozy Gray", *New York Times* (6 February), AR4, 16.

Nightingale, Benedict (2001), "Any port in a storm of lost love", *The Times* (24 February), www.newsint-archive. co.uk.

Nowlan, David (2001), "Port Authority", *Irish Times* (24 February), www.ireland.com.

O'Toole, Fintan (1997), "I'm relieved I was wrong", *Irish Times* (19 August), www.ireland.com.

O'Toole, Fintan (1998), "Shadows Over Ireland", *American Theatre*, 15 (July), 16–19.

O'Toole, Fintan (2000), "Play for Ireland", *Irish Times* (12 February), www.ireland.com.

O'Toole, Fintan (2001), "Getting back to the story", *Irish Times* (12 October), www.ireland.com.

Power, Paul (1997), "The Fine Art of Surfacing", *Film West*, 30 (October), 16–19.

Power, Paul (1999), "The Irish Are Rising Again: Profiles of New Filmmaking Talent", *Cineaste*, vol. 24, nos. 2-3 (March), 74–75.

Renner, Pamela (2001), "The Good Thief", *Variety*, 382 (16–22 April), 38.

Riding, Alan (1997), "The Arts Find Fertile Ground in a Flourishing Ireland", *New York Times* (21 December), AR1, 40.

Rooney, David (2000), "Endgame", *Variety* (9 October), 30.

Rothstein, Mervyn (2003), "The Subject Is Fear and the Excesses It Breeds" (16 February), www.nytimes.com.

Russo, Francine (1998), "Brit Crit", *Village Voice*, 43 (7 April), 96.

Saltwater, The Press Release, Buena Vista International, 29 September 2000.

Scallan, Anne (1998), "Non Places — Irish Cinema From Another Perspective", *Film West*, 32 (May), 22–24.

Scholem, Richard (1999), "The Weir", *Long Island Business News* 46 (12 February), 25A.

Shea, Lisa (1999), "The Supernaturalist", *Elle* (1 April), 194.

Shirley, Don (2003), "Soloing, but not in song", *Los Angeles Times* (21 January), E3.

Shore, Robert (2001), "Port Authority", *Times Literary Supplement* 5111 (16 March), 19.

Simon, John (1999a), "Blarney's Tone", *New York* (12 April), 84.

Simon, John (1999b), "Bower Play", *New York* 32 (31 May), 99–100.

Simon, John (1998), "Sweet and Sour", *New York* 31 (30 March), 63, 65.

Singleton, Brian (2001), "Am I Talking To Myself?", *Irish Times* (24 April), www.ireland.com.

Smythe, Simon (2001), "Conor McPherson", *Newsnight Review* (23 February), www.bbc.co.uk.

Soloski, Alexis (2002), "War, Women, and Booze", *Village Voice*, vol. 47, no. 43 (23–29 October), 65.

Stokes, John (2000), "Back in the Habit", *Times Literary Supplement* (3 March), 20.

Stratton, David (2000), "Saltwater", *Variety* (6 March), 40.

Susman, Gary (1998), "Fresh Eire", *Village Voice*, 43 (30 June), 138.

Trevor, William (1989), "Introduction", *The Oxford Book of Irish Short Stories*, New York: Oxford UP.

Walpole, Rob, and Paddy Breathnach (1997), "Two Went Down", *Film Ireland* (August/September), 12–13.

Weinert, Laura (2001), "The Weir", *Back Stage West*, 8 (15 February), 12.

White, Victoria (1994), "Love's small steps to ruin," *Irish Times* (27 August), 14.

White, Victoria (2000), "Front row", *Irish Times* (23 March), www.ireland.com.

Whitehead, Sam (1998a), "*St Nicholas*", *Time Out New York* (2–9 April), www.timeoutny.com.

Whitehead, Sam (1998b), "*The Weir*", *Time Out New York* (8–15 April), www.timeoutny.com.

Whitehead, Sam (1998c), "*This Lime Tree Bower*", *Time Out New York* (27 May – 2 June), www.timeoutny.com.

Wolf, Matt (1997), "The Weir" *Variety*, 367 (4–10 August), 43.

Wolf, Matt (1998b), "Count your blessings", *Variety*, 369 (5 January), 83.

Wolf, Matt (1999a), "Royal Court Gets a Regal Revamp", *Variety* (27 September – 3 October), 155, 157.

Wolf, Matt (1999b), "They Also Act Who Only Sit and Listen", *New York Times* (13 June), 9, 24.

Wolf, Matt (2000), "Dublin Carol", *Variety*, 377 (31 January – 6 February), 44.

Wolf, Matt (2001), "Port Authority", *Variety*, (19 March), www.variety.com.

Wren, Celia (1998), "Saint Nicholas", *Commonweal* (8 May), 15–16.

Wren, Celia (1999), "The Weir", *Commonweal* (4 June), 21–22.

Index